Creating a Successful

Nonprofit

by knowing the

NUMBERS

A Guide for Nonprofit Founders and Board Members

By

Rolanda S. McDuffie CPA

ISBN: 978-1-7375815-0-5

Contents

INTRODUCTION 1

TAX-EXEMPT ORGANIZATION DEFINED 3

ORGANIZATION ELIGIBILITY 4
APPLYING FOR TAX-EXEMPT STATUS 5

GOVERNING PROCEDURES FOR NONPROFITS 8

NONPROFITS' GOVERNING DOCUMENTS AND POLICIES 9

POLICIES AND PROCEDURES FOR GOVERNING 9

GOVERNANCE POLICIES ALL NONPROFIT NEED 15

GOVERNANCE POLICIES AND TYPES 16

BOARD MEMBER ROLES AND RESPONSIBILITIES 19

POLICYMAKING'S FUNCTION 20
THE ROLE OF DECISION MAKING 20
THE ROLE OF OVERSIGHT 21

BOARD MEMBERS' FIDUCIARY RESPONSIBILITY 23

THE TERM "FIDUCIARY" DEFINED. 23
UNDERSTANDING THE BASIC FINANCIAL STATEMENTS 26
SETTING UP AND MONITORING KEY FINANCIAL INDICATORS 26
ENSURING ADEQUATE CONTROL FUNCTIONS 27
APPROVING THE BUDGET 27
OVERSEEING THE ORGANIZATION'S LEGAL OBLIGATIONS 28

EFFECTIVE BOARD GOVERNANCE OVERSIGHT 32

THE DUTY OF BOARD MEMBERS TO OVERSEE FINANCIAL
OPERATIONS 36

FUNDAMENTALS OF A BOARD DEVELOPMENT COMMITTEE 42

ROLES AND RESPONSIBILITIES OF NONPROFIT FINANCE
COMMITTEE 46

THE FINANCE COMMITEE OBLIGATION 48

FINANCIAL PLANNING AND BUDGETING 48
CREATING FINANCIAL REPORTS 49
INTERNAL CONTROLS AND POLICIES OF ACCOUNTABILITY 50
PERSONNEL GUIDELINES 51
COMMITTEE OF AUDITORS 52
COMMITTEE ON INVESTMENTS 52
THE FINANCE COMMITTEE CHAIR'S FUNCTION 53

IRS RULES CONCERNING DONATIONS 55

ISSUANCE OF TAX-COMPLIANT DONATION RECEIPT..............................55
QUID PRO QUO CONTRIBUTIONS 57

IN-KIND DONATIONS AND FINANCIAL STATEMENTS 61

RECORDING IN-KIND GIFTS 61
TIMING OF RECORDING IN-KIND GIFTS TO NONPROFIT ORGANIZATIONS 62
THE VALUATION PROCESS FOR IN-KIND DONATIONS 62
ACKNOWLEDGMENT OF IN-KIND DONATIONS: FORMALLY AND INFORMALLY
.... 63
TRACKING DONATIONS AND ACKNOWLEDGMENTS 65

PAYING THE STAFF 66

PAYROLL TAX LIABILITY 67
EMPLOYEES OR INDEPENDENT CONTRACTORS................................. 68
BOARD MEMBERS COMPENSATION... 69
LEGAL IMPLICATIONS WITH PAYING BOARD MEMBERS 70
PAYING THE EXECUTIVE DIRECTOR 70
PAYING BOARD MEMBERS 71
DETERMINING BOARD MEMBERS PAY 73
BOARD OF DIRECTOR'S REIMBURSEMENT 74

REASONABLE COMPENSATION DEFINED 75

TRAINING NONPROFIT BOARD MEMBERS TO READ AND UNDERSTAND FINANCIAL REPORTS 76

THE FOLLOWING ARE SOME EXAMPLES OF COMMON FINANCIAL REPORTS:...... 76

REASONS ACCOUNTING IS IMPORTANT............................ 81

ESTABLISHING A BUDGET...83

BUDGETING TIPS NONPROFITS SHOULD FOLLOW 86

FINANCIAL OVERSIGHT – WHY NONPROFIT BOARDS NEED TO REVIEW MORE THAN THE OPERATING BUDGET.......................... 90

THE UNIQUENESS OF NONPROFITS ACCOUNTING 92

FUND ACCOUNTING DEFINED 94
OVERVIEW OF FINANCIAL STATEMENTS 98

DIFFERENCES BETWEEN ACCOUNTING FOR NONPROFITS AND FOR-PROFITS.. 104

BENEFITS OF USING ACCOUNTING SOFTWARE.......................... 107

NONPROFITS' NEED FOR ACCOUNTANTS................................110

DIFFERENCE BETWEEN AN AUDIT, REVIEW, AND COMPILATION 114

AUDIT... 114
REVIEW 116

COMPILATION.. 116
IS AN AUDIT NECESSARY?.. 117
WAYS AUDIT SERVICES BENEFIT YOUR NONPROFIT 118

THE IMPORTANCE OF ADHERING TO REGULATORY REQUIREMENTS 121

FORM 990 DEFINED 124

FORM 990 AND HOW IT WORKS..126

WHAT NONPROFIT BOARD MEMBERS SHOULD KNOW ABOUT FORM 990 130

CHARITIES THAT ARE REQUIRED TO FILE A FORM 990......................... 131
FORM 990 (FULL FORM)... 132
FORM 990-EZ.. 134
FORM 990-N.. 137

UNRELATED BUSINESS TAXABLE INCOME DEFINED..................141

REPORTING OF CORPORATE SPONSORSHIPS.. 146

THE IMPORTANCE OF THE TIMELINESS OF FORM 990 151

FINES AND PENALTIES.. 152
REINSTATING A NONPROFIT'S 501(C)3 EXEMPTION STATUS RETROACTIVE..... 154

ORGANIZATIONAL RISK MANAGEMENT...157

KEEPING THE NONPROFIT'S ASSETS SAFE 160

PHYSICAL ASSETS 160
CASH ASSETS 161

UNDERSTANDING A NONPROFIT'S FINANCIAL HEALTH...........167

CONCLUSION..169

APPENDICES 172

APPENDIX A: SAMPLE CONFLICT OF INTEREST POLICY.................... 173
APPENDIX B: DONOR ACKNOWLEDGEMENT TEMPLATES............. 180
APPENDIX C: COMPENSATION POLICY FOR OFFICERS, DIRECTORS, TOP MANAGEMENT OFFICIAL AND KEY EMPLOYEES..................... 184
APPENDIX D: SAMPLE WHISTLEBLOWER POLICY 190
APPENDIX E: EXPENSE REIMBURSEMENT POLICY............................ 193
APPENDIX F: BOARD OF DIRECTORS AND FINANCE COMMITTEE OVERSIGHT CHECKLIST 196
APPENDIX G: DOCUMENT RETENTION POLICY................................ 200
APPENDIX H: EXAMPLE NONPROFIT FINANCIAL STATEMENTS . 203

ABOUT THE AUTHOR 207

INTRODUCTION

When starting a nonprofit organization, founders and boards of directors become so overwhelmed with the process and paperwork required. However, the paperwork, number crunching, and other dull responsibilities come with the accountability of running an effective nonprofit organization. One of the many activities with which many nonprofit organizations don't want to deal is the nonprofit's numbers. This consists of budgets, payroll, donation compliance, nonprofit accounting, and Form 990.

However, one of the core areas in which nonprofits need to excel is accounting and finance. Not only is this essential to a nonprofit's organization operations, the numbers provide transparency for donors and funders. The nonprofit's numbers serve as the basis upon which accountability and mission effectiveness will be measured.

More importantly, it does not matter what your organization's mission is, good accounting of your numbers is always critical to its sustainability and whether it can fulfill its ultimate objective. Accurate accounting records are especially important for nonprofits, which frequently have to stretch every dollar for key programs.

Nonprofit accounting is a unique method through which nonprofits plan, record, and report their finances. Nonprofit accounting makes use of specialized terminology and classifications to keep track of what activities are being supported and to provide reports that show donors how their money is being spent. Nonprofit organizations have a specific set of rules and procedures to follow that help them stay accountable to their contributors and donors. Nonprofit accounting is focused on transparency and for-profits accounting is focused on net profits earned.

Nonprofits accounting can be tricky. Tax requirements for nonprofits are rigorous, and can be difficult to track all of the variable funding sources. Fortunately, with the right accounting policies and procedures, compliance and accountability can be tracked through the nonprofit organization's financials.

In this book, we'll review the fundamentals and best practices that all nonprofit board of directors and finance committee members should know about their numbers. Understanding the fundamentals will help to manage and plan programs in a way that brings the most value from the finances while keeping the organization compliant and accountable to stakeholders and the general public.

TAX-EXEMPT ORGANIZATION DEFINED

A nonprofit organization is a private and legal organization that is established for the public and social benefit. The Internal Revenue Service (IRS) defines a nonprofit organization as "an entity that is organized and operated exclusively for tax-exempt purposes." Nonprofit organizations have no owners and have a goal that isn't just about making money. It's an entity with the primary objective of using all of its funds for the achievement of the organization's mission. It collects funds from donors and uses them to maximize the achievements of the organization's objectives. The IRS also requires that nonprofits do not distribute earnings to any private shareholder or individual.

The term nonprofit has been misunderstood to mean that the organization maintains a financial loss. However, to sustain, an organization's revenues must exceed its expenses to support operations. Therefore, the difference between a for-profit and nonprofit in this area is how the organization uses surplus revenue. Tax-exempt entities work for a social cause and they do not exist to earn profits for their owners; instead, all funds are used for the social cause and organization mission. Tax-exempt nonprofit organizations include those established for religious, spiritual, educational, charitable, scientific, literary reasons, fostering national/international amateur sports competition, preventing cruelty to children/animals and testing for public safety.

Some of the well-known and successful non-profit organizations include:

- Boys & Girls Club of America
- Habitat for Humanity
- United Way

In support of nonprofits, the IRS provides tax benefits to the organizations by allowing them to apply for tax-exempt status under section 501(c)(3) of the Internal Revenue Code.

If an organization is tax-exempted, it usually does not have to pay tax on the donations that it receives.

Organization eligibility

To determine if your organization is eligible for the exemption status under section 501(c)(3), the organization must be established for the following reasons:

- religious
- spiritual
- educational
- charitable
- scientific
- literary reasons

- fostering national or international amateur sports competition
- preventing cruelty to children or animals
- testing for public safety.

It is important to note that an organization will not be treated as described in section 501(c)(3) unless the IRS has been notified through your application. This, however, does not apply to churches; or their integrated auxiliaries whose annual gross receipts are usually less than $5,000.

If your organization needs to apply for this recognition of exemption, you must inform the IRS within 27 months from the date your organization is formed, to be treated as described in section 501(c)(3) from the date formed.

It is important to note that the IRS has strict measures for the extent that organizations under section 501(c)(3) can take part in political and legislative activities. Therefore, if your organization participates in any political activity, you have to ensure that it is nonpartisan in nature.

Applying for tax-exempt status

In order to qualify for the tax-exempt status, an organization will have to submit a Form 1023-series application. The IRS is no longer accepting Form 1023 paper submissions as of April 30, 2020. This application has to be submitted via www.pay.gov electronically and a user fee will be payable.

Smaller nonprofits may be eligible to file Form 1023-EZ, Streamlined Application for Recognition of Exemption Under Section 501(c)(3) of the Internal Revenue Code. This is a shorter, simpler application form that can be completed online. Form 1023-EZ may only be filed by nonprofits with less than $50,000 in annual receipts and $250,000 in total assets. The filing fee is also much less than the long form.

The full Form 1023, Application for Recognition of Exemption Under Section 501(c)(3) of the Internal Revenue Code, is divided into 11 parts and is much more detailed than the streamlined version of the form. If an organization's annual receipts and assets exceed the amount allowed to complete the streamlined Form 1023-EZ, more than $50,000 in annual receipts and $250,000 in total assets, the full Form 1023 must be completed.

A charity's organizing document must limit the organization's purposes to exempt purposes set forth in section 501(c)(3) and must not expressly empower it to engage, other than as an insubstantial part of its activities, in ventures that do not further those purposes. This requirement may be met if the purposes stated in the organizing document are limited by reference to section 501(c)(3) which are outlined above.

In addition, an organization's assets must be permanently used for its established exempt purpose. This means that if an organization dissolves, its assets must be distributed for an exempt purpose described in section 501(c)(3), or to the federal government or to a state or local government for a public purpose. To establish that an organization's assets will be permanently used for an exempt purpose, the organizing document should contain a provision insuring their distribution for an exempt purpose if the organization dissolves.

Once the application has been approved, the application for recognition of exemption with all supporting documents and the last three annual information returns must be made available for public inspection.

Except for a reasonable fee for printing costs, an organization must also provide copies of these documents upon request without charge. Failure to comply with the requirements can result in penalties for the organization.

Forming a nonprofit includes completing many legal documents, including, the state's incorporation paperwork and the Internal Revenue Service's Form 1023. While these forms can be filled out by board members, consider hiring an experienced attorney or Certified Public Accountant (CPA) to complete the forms, or at least review them before being submitted for approval.

GOVERNING PROCEDURES FOR
NONPROFITS

The IRS generally requires every nonprofit organization to have a minimum of three board members, but does not dictate a maximum number of members. The board members term length is not determined by the IRS. Service term lengths must be outlined in the nonprofit's bylaws. Typically, board service terms are one to five years; they aren't intended to be perpetual. New board members are usually nominated and a vote is taken by existing board members in traditional organizations; and by stakeholders vote in nonprofits that operate via membership.

The IRS expects (and state law usually dictates) that a board of directors should meet a minimum of once a year, and the industry's best practices recommend four times a year. During these meetings, the annual budget is passed, the IRS Form 990 is approved, and operational and strategic decisions requiring votes are discussed. It is important to remember that the board of directors is responsible for the governance of the nonprofit, not the management. The day-to-day management of the nonprofit is the responsibility of the Executive Director.

NONPROFITS' GOVERNING DOCUMENTS AND POLICIES

As new boards of directors' gain experience in their roles, they rapidly realize nonprofit board of directors' responsibility. An enormous number of regulations and procedures alone is enough to keep you occupied for many hours. The advantage of having clear and accessible policies and processes means everything is controlled in a consistent manner. Nonprofit rules and procedures ensure the organization responds to all situations fairly and equitably.

Policies and procedures serve as a guide for employees, volunteers, and the board of directors.

Nonprofit rules and procedures can have an impact on a variety of aspects of a nonprofit's operations that includes: governance, employee behavior, employee benefits, and anything else that has to be written properly.

Policies and Procedures for Governing

To stay in conformity with laws and regulations, nonprofits are required by the government to complete and register essential organizational documents. Although organizational documents are not policies and procedures in and of themselves, it is necessary to preserve them online so that the board of directors can easily access them when expressing the organization's mission and initiatives. The mission statement, bylaws, Articles of Incorporation, and organizational chart are among these documents. These are the key documents that explain why the organization was founded.

Policies of the Board of Directors

The types of rules that a nonprofit should develop will differ significantly, depending on the type and size of the organization. Conflict of interest, whistleblower, code of ethics, anti-harassment, and data retention and destruction are only a few of the core nonprofit rules and procedures.

Policy on Conflicts of Interest

A conflict of interest is an activity or interest that might lead to a lack of objectivity in the board of directors' examination of a particular transaction. A conflict-of-interest policy is used to assist all members of your nonprofit in identifying, disclosing, and dealing with financial or other conflicts of interest. This is a policy that all nonprofits, regardless of size, should have. To ensure that boards make decisions fairly, the IRS requires nonprofit boards to adopt a conflict-of-interest policy. See Appendix A for an example of this policy.

Policy on Whistleblowers

Whistleblower policies encourage employees to report financial and other irregularities by developing mechanisms to protect whistleblowers from retaliation and keeping their identities hidden. The whistleblower policy's objective is to prevent an employee from being fired if they choose to report misconduct within the organization.

In addition, whistleblower rules are used to prevent fraud in all types of organizations. The policy should include a defined procedure for dealing with employee or volunteer complaints, as well as any concerns about retaliation against the reporting employee. This is definitely unnecessary for a small organization with no staff. See Appendix D for an example of this policy.

Retention and destruction of records

Nonprofit organizations must also have a formal documents preservation and disposal policy, which is under the Sarbanes-Oxley Act. The Act was enacted in response to several major corporate and accounting scandals that raised questions about accountability. Even if your organization isn't subject to Sarbanes-Oxley, having a records' retention and disposal policy is a smart idea. Record keeping is also a prerequisite for getting funds under state and federal laws. This is a fantastic policy to have in place for all nonprofits.

Nonprofit auditors should make sure that organizations are complying with state and federal grant requirements. This record-retention policy outlines how long nonprofit's records must be retained before being destroyed. All documents should be kept for at least three years, and in certain circumstances even longer. See Appendix G for further information about the duration of retention for specific documents.

Code of Ethics

A nonprofit's behavior and decisions are governed by ethical principles outlined in the code of ethics. The code in a nonprofit organization pertains to the board of directors, management, employees, and volunteers. The code of ethics becomes woven into the fabric of the organization's culture.

Harassment Prevention

Harassment can take many forms that includes: physical, verbal, emotional, and sexual; and it may take place in any context, including the boardroom. Nonprofit leaders should be proactive in preventing and responding to all forms of harassment. For failing to safeguard employees and volunteers from harassment, illegal discrimination, or retribution for reporting any sort of harassment, nonprofit boards may incur legal liability.

Other Policies and Procedures to Consider in Nonprofits

Employees and volunteers are subject to many other policies and procedures. Combining policies and procedures into an employee or volunteer manual is the simplest approach to deliver the information. The manual's recipients should acknowledge receipt of the manual in writing.

Having a policy on internet usage, organization equipment usage, and social media usage is a noteworthy problem that nonprofits should examine in today's world. Employees and volunteers may be required to use the nonprofit's internet service to carry out many of their daily tasks. Employees and volunteers must be clear about how they may use the internet during work or volunteer hours. Nonprofits should also keep an eye on internet usage and make sure that they have the right passwords for the sites they're allowed to use.

Equal opportunity employment, anti-discrimination, disciplinary procedures, overtime regulations, weekend compensation, and flextime are all topics for which nonprofit boards should consider when adopting rules and procedures. The board should also think about things such as, drugs, drinking, smoking, safety, and dress code.

Benefits are another area where nonprofits could focus. Written policy on vacation, sick leave, holidays and religious observances, medical leave, maternity leave, personal time, and bereavement should be provided to employees and volunteers.

Nonprofits that provide health benefits to their employees should provide written information on medical, dental, COBRA, life and disability insurance, and workers' compensation.

Having an accounting policies and procedures manual in your organization is helpful to document the principles and policies governing your organization's accounting practices.

The accounting policies and policies provide:

- A foundation for a system of internal controls.
- Guidance in current financial activities.
- Criteria for decisions on appropriate accounting treatment.

- Board of Directors with direction and guidance in connection with those accounting transactions, procedures, and reports that should be uniform throughout the organization.

When consistently applied, these policies and policies guarantee that the various financial statements issued by the organization accurately reflect the results of the nonprofit's operations. Internal controls provide a system of checks and balances intended to identify irregularities; prevent waste, fraud, and abuse from occurring; and assist in resolving discrepancies that are accidentally introduced into the operations of the business.

Accessibility of Policies and Procedures

Written policies and procedures are simply one aspect of the communication process for ensuring that programs and activities run smoothly and efficiently. The board should ensure that those rules and procedures are properly communicated to staff, volunteers, and board members as part of their oversight responsibilities, so that everyone is aware of and understands the expectations.

Afterward, staff and volunteers should be trained on policies and procedures, and frequent evaluations should be conducted to ensure that everyone is following them. The policies and procedures should be reviewed at least once a year by the board of directors.

GOVERNANCE POLICIES ALL NONPROFIT NEED

To help prevent abuses, the IRS strongly urges organizations to adopt specific types of governance practices. These principles, according to the IRS, are "hallmarks of a well-governed organization," and a charity that lacks them is "more vulnerable to persons who would utilize it for their personal benefit or to participate in nonexempt activities."

The IRS strongly encourages, but does not require, the implementation of these rules. Of course, the IRS lacks the jurisdiction to enforce such a requirement because governance issues are generally governed by state nonprofit corporation law rather than IRS-administered federal tax law. Nonetheless, IRS officials have stated that organizations that do not adopt specific practices are more likely to be audited than those that do, with the logic that organizations that adopt the practices are more likely to be in compliance with tax law.

A series of questions on IRS Form 990, the yearly information return filed by larger organizations, asks if your organization has implemented particular rules. A string of "no" responses in this portion of the Form does not appeal to the general public who reads the result.

You do not, however, have to follow all of the proposed policies. Whether a certain policy, process, or practice should be implemented by an organization may depend on the organization's size, type, and culture, according to the Form 990 guidelines. As a result, it's critical that each organization think about the governance policies and practices that are most appropriate to ensure solid operations and compliance.

Governance Policies and Types

A board meeting should be held to review major policies already adopted within the nonprofit and determine if any of the following policies should be adopted or revised.

Policy on repayment of expenses.

The IRS and the public are divided on whether or not nonprofit officers, directors, trustees, and key employees should be reimbursed or paid for their expenditures. A separate Schedule J on Form 990 deals mostly with this topic: If a nonprofit reimburses or pays officers, directors, trustees, and key employees for first-class or charter travel, companion travel, tax gross-up payments (payment of any taxes owed on taxable benefits such as travel), discretionary expenditures, lodging, health or social club dues, and such personal services as the use of a chauffeur, the schedule specifically asks. If a nonprofit reimbursed or paid any officers, directors, trustees, and key employees for any of these expenses, it must be declared that there is a documented policy in place. An explanation is required if there isn't a documented policy in place.

Policy on joint ventures.

This policy requires a nonprofit to identify, report, and manage joint ventures—that is, partnerships with for-profit companies. Smaller nonprofits aren't usually participating in such endeavors.

Policy on accepting gifts.

Non-standard contributions are reviewed, accepted, and substantiated according to a gift-acceptance policy. Contributions of assets that are difficult to sell and/or value, such as vacation timeshares or stock in a privately held corporation, are examples. If your nonprofit receives such unusual donations, you should implement a policy like this.

Policies for chapters, branches, and affiliates.

This policy is only required if a nonprofit has local chapters, branches, or affiliates.

Sample Policies and Procedures

If one or more of the recommended governance policies is needed, the board of directors will need to write a policy and get it approved by the majority of the board of directors. There is no one-size- fits-all approach to writing any of the policies required or suggested previously. The policies and procedures for an organization can be simple or complicated.

Sample policies in a variety of sources can be found via various sources. The appendix of this book features a number of sample documents that can be used. In addition, we also offer additional resources that can be downloaded, for a modest price, from our website at *www.rsmcduffiecpa.com/nonprofit.*

BOARD MEMBER ROLES AND RESPONSIBILITIES

Many obligations, qualities, and responsibilities lie under the umbrella of items that board of directors should possess. Governance is a broad term that encompasses all of a board's functions. Because governance pervades every board decision, it's critical that every board of directors grasp what governance is and what defines good governance.

The board exists only when it comes together as one body. It only has one voice when it speaks. The dynamics vary with each new board of director who enters and exits the board. The board may only have 24 hours of total time together, regardless of who fills the seats in the boardroom. That implies it must work efficiently and effectively to manage its time.

Effective governance is a solid basis that gives board members a firm foundation. Good governance paves the way for productive and courteous conversations on difficult issues. When a board works well together, it creates synergy and positive results. Boards must be aware of the extensive number of stakeholders, that demand their ability to be integrative. Boards serve as important providers in the community and contribute to the preservation of the community's assets.

Despite the complexities and obstacles of sitting on a board, it is a position that can be enjoyable and rewarding on a personal level.

To summarize, the board's role can be divided into three areas. It is in charge of setting policies, making strategic decisions, and monitoring organizational activity. There's always space for improvement, no matter what abilities, talents, or expertise that member brings to their board.

Policymaking's Function

Decision making and oversight are aided by good policies. They aid in the separation of duties among the board, management, and staff. Good policies enable you to avoid having the same items on the agenda at every meeting. Policies provide clarity and once written and approved, the board can delegate implementation to management.

The Code of Ethics is one of the board's most essential policies. This policy spells out what it will and will not accept. Because actions speak louder than words, board of directors should be mindful of their professional and personal behavior.

With the fast speed of business, it's also a good idea for boards to evaluate their policies once a year to make sure they're still relevant and current.

The Role of Decision Making

The board has a decision-making role when it comes to the organization's purpose, goals, and strategies. Regardless of the size of the organization, boards are responsible for making critical and strategic decisions.

The Role of Oversight

An organization's board of directors is legally liable for everything that occurs. Their responsibilities include overseeing all aspect of the organization.

Delegating key responsibilities to committees and ensuring that all participants have the right credentials are other methods they can use to achieve quality assurance. Because committees play such a crucial part in the governance process, the board of directors should examine their structure and activities on a regular basis and clarify the committees' responsibilities.

The board of directors must maintain strong community links in addition to providing monitoring. One of their most significant responsibilities is to find, attract, appoint, and supervise the Executive Director. If the Executive Director fails to fulfil his or her responsibilities, the board of directors has the authority to terminate him or her and must select a replacement.

While the Executive Director and senior executives create the day-to-day plan, it is up to the board of directors to approve it or request changes. Many factors go into forming the ultimate plan, including assessing the community needs and keeping up with the ever-changing landscape. The board must make sure that the strategic and day-to-day plan are in line with the organization's vision, purpose, values, and goals.

Compliance is one of the more recent obligations that boards must accomplish. Board of directors who do not follow government requirements risk being fined and may be imprisoned.

Respect is a necessary attribute for all board of directors, and they must demonstrate it in a variety of situations, including their interactions with other directors, management, clinicians, employees, and the organization as a whole. When directors are combative, it is distracting, unproductive, and produces toxicity in the workplace that can spread like a virus. Board of directors must have a degree of openness and complete confidentiality in addition to possessing and demonstrating respect.

Financial supervision is a common task at which most boards excel. Boards must ensure that the organization's internal financial controls are in place and that money is invested properly. Boards must assess how they manage their cash flow, banking systems, and contracts, as well as develop policies relating to their budgets, in their function as policymakers.

BOARD MEMBERS' FIDUCIARY RESPONSIBILITY

One of the main responsibilities of board members is to maintain financial accountability of their organization.

Board members act as trustees of the organization's assets and must exercise due diligence and oversight to ensure that the organization is well managed and that its financial situation remains sound.

The Term "Fiduciary" Defined.

When a nonprofit organization is founded, a group of people will be tasked with the responsibility to run the organization. They are known as the board of directors. Directors participate in the administration, guidance, and supervision of the affairs of an organization.

Once the directors are appointed, they have the responsibility to ensure the sustainability of the organization, good governance, and make sure that the organization has the resources to carry out its missions.

Based on what is mentioned above, the directors of nonprofit organizations have a very important role to play. They are entrusted with the responsibilities to always act in the best interest of the organization, even when such an act contradicts their self-interests. This is called a "fiduciary responsibility."

The term "fiduciary" is a legal term and it refers to a person who has the responsibility to act primarily for another's benefit because of the position he or she holds. Fiduciary duties are enforceable by law and their existence is to protect those who are vulnerable from those who hold power.

Fiduciary duty requires board members to stay objective, unselfish, responsible, honest, trustworthy, and efficient. Board members, as stewards of public trust, must always act for the good of the organization, rather than for the benefit of themselves. They need to exercise reasonable care in all decision making, without placing the organization under unnecessary risk.

A nonprofit's board of directors are usually, but not always, protected from personal liability for lawsuits against the nonprofit. However, in a few instances, board of directors can be held personally liable for the nonprofit's debts. A board of director or officer of a nonprofit organization can be held personally liable if he or she:

- Personally and directly injures someone.
- Personally guarantees a bank loan or a business debt in which the corporation defaults.
- Fails to ensure that the nonprofit deposits taxes (such as payroll and property taxes) or files necessary tax returns.
- Does something intentionally fraudulent, illegal, or clearly unreasonable that causes harm, or

- Co-mingles nonprofit and personal funds.

The cost of a board member failing at their fiduciary duty depends on the situation, and the expected level of responsibility any one board member should have. To cover some, but not all, of these situations, reasonably priced insurance is accessible to protect the nonprofit and its volunteer directors and officers.

A nonprofit's unpaid taxes can cause the biggest risk to board members' liability. A deteriorating nonprofit may find itself unable to pay taxes, and then shuts down. After the organization is liquidated, the IRS may turn to the board of directors for payment, and the board members may discover that their insurance doesn't cover unpaid taxes.

The IRS can also hold board members personally liable for penalties for allowing excess private benefit to occur. This usually involves unreasonable compensation to someone who is both a board member and an employee. It could also happen if the board decides to do business with another board member's business without properly allowing for competing alternatives in the process. These situations are considered inurement and are prohibited, and fines are levied directly against the board of director, not the charity. The IRS can go as high as 200% of the amount of excess benefit. It is wise for every board to ensure due diligence is exercised when any type of money is being paid to another board member or officer.

Understanding the basic financial statements

Not every board member can be a financial wizard. Every board member, however, needs to be a financial investigator. It is essential to understand basic terminology, be able to read financial statements and judge their soundness, and have the capacity to recognize warning signs that might indicate a change in the overall health of the organization. If a board member does not understand something, he or she must be willing to find the answer.

Setting up and monitoring key financial indicators

Having the proper tools to monitor and evaluate financial performance strengthens the board's capacity to judge the health of the organization. Board members need to agree on general guidelines and standards to measure the effectiveness of organizational accomplishments. Appropriate policies must be in place to guide management and board decision making.

Specific questions board members should ask:

- Is our financial plan consistent with our strategic plan?
- Is our cash flow projected to be adequate to cover expenses?
- Do we have sufficient cash reserves?
- Are any specific expense areas rising faster than their sources of income?

- Are we regularly comparing our financial activity with what we have budgeted?

- Are our expenses appropriate?

- Do we have the appropriate checks and balances to prevent errors, fraud, and abuse?

- Are we meeting guidelines and requirements set by our funders?

Ensuring adequate control functions

Control functions are not intended to detect fraud, but rather to prevent it. Ensuring clarity in job descriptions and responsibilities; defining financial and accounting procedures (signing checks, handling cash, approving expenses, outlining parameters for credit card usage); managing potential conflicts of interest with a clear policy; and requesting regular external audits are all manifestations of fiduciary responsibility.

Approving the budget

The budget creates the framework for program management and overall administrative decisions. The annual budget approval process helps curb any tendency for the board to micromanage. Securing necessary funding is part of a viable budget. Examining financial statements regularly and comparing actual figures to the projected statements allow the board to verify that the general guidelines stay on track. The board should question any major variances.

Overseeing the organization's legal obligations

The board verifies that all filing requirements and tax obligations are completed. The organization must prepare Form 990 completely and file it on time. It must regularly withhold and pay employment taxes. To avoid any issues or penalties, the board must document and justify its executive compensation and any financial transactions.

All board of directors of nonprofit organizations must understand their fiduciary duties well, which include the following:

Duty of Care

A duty of care is a legal obligation imposed on an individual. It requires the individual to exercise reasonable care while conducting acts that could foreseeably harm the benefits of other parties. In simpler terms, it is an obligation to take care of the safety or well-being of others.

Act with competence

The directors should act with a standard level of skill and care expected of a person in their profession or position. Note, there is no requirement for the directors to be experts.

Act with diligence

The board of directors must devote sufficient time to do their duties. They should also be reasonably informed of an issue before making any business decision related to it.

Act with accountability

As a board of directors, they must provide all information to the members of the nonprofit organizations and be accountable to them for all funds raised and collected.

Act with no delegation

The board of directors are usually selected for their personal qualities and abilities. It is therefore vital that they perform the tasks of a director themselves and not delegate to anyone else.

However, there is an exception to this. Delegations may be required to ensure the task is carried out in the best interests of the organization. For example, the directors may instruct a professional valuer to value the organization's assets to ensure they can be sold at their highest values.

Act with obedience

Directors must act strictly in accordance with all applicable laws and the organization's governing documents. They should ensure that the organizations are abiding by all relevant laws and regulations and do not engage in any activities that are unauthorized or breach the laws.

An example to demonstrate:

Angel holds a degree in nonprofit management. She is currently an Executive Director in Company RED and has recently accepted the role of an Executive Director in Charity BLUE (*act with competence*).

Although there is another offer for her to act as a director in a listed company, she rejected it because she wants to ensure that she is able to give sufficient levels of attention to both organizations (*act with diligence*).

Upon her selection of Nonprofit BLUE, Angel realized that her nephew is one of the recipients. She had immediately disclosed the relationship to the organizations (*act with accountability*).

She always gets involved when it comes to handling major day-to-day matters of the organization (*act with no delegation*) and makes sure that the organization engages in activities that comply with the relevant laws and regulations (*act with obedience*).

Duty of loyalty

The duty of loyalty is also known as the fundamental principle of fiduciary relationships.

Act with no conflict of interest

The directors should act in the interest of the non-profit organization and not put themselves in a situation where their own interest conflicts with those of the organization.

Act with confidence

It is important that the directors keep in confidence what they know of the affairs of those under their care when exercising their duty as directors. This is even applicable after the directors have ceased working for the organization.

Act with honesty

The directors should deal honestly with the organization and in good faith for the best interests of the organization. They must not act for an inappropriate purpose.

An example to illustrate:

Mark is the director of a nonprofit organization whose mission is to help children with special needs. One of its projects is to help build hospitals that can accommodate the needs of such children.

Mark also runs a construction company. To avoid conflict of interest, he decided not to tender for the new projecto build a hospital (*act with no conflict of interest*).

Despite knowing the budget of the project and the tender prices submitted by other contractors, he did not disclose it to his good friend who is also tendering for the project (*act with confidence*).

Mark's own construction business is doing very well and he knows that he can no longer commit the time required of him for the nonprofit organization. He immediately informs the chairman of his situation and subsequently resigns from his position (*act with honesty*).

EFFECTIVE BOARD GOVERNANCE
OVERSIGHT

Many of the definitions of Board Governance are broad and theoretical. But when I consult with boards that are interested in improving their ability to govern, I use a more practical definition that includes six keys to good governance. Additionally, I provide a few examples of actions or evidence that support each of the six focus areas. These focus areas, with their examples, helps board members learn how to work more effectively with their executive director and staff, and provide proper and thorough oversight to the organization they lead.

Here are the six keys to good board governance – and some examples that will help to implement board governance more effectively.

1. Ensure that the organization is adhering to its mission.
    a. There's a crisp, clear mission statement for the organization.
    b. All of the projects that are not within the scope of this mission statement are eliminated.
    c. If any potential funding or programs fall outside of the mission, they are discussed thoroughly and need to be approved by the board.

2. Approve and follow a strategy for the organization.
   a. Be sure the organization has a strategy (a minimum of three years out).
   b. Know how the organization is evolving and why.
   c. Agree on the key milestones that are expected to be achieved and their due dates.
   d. Debate thoroughly all funding, programs, or projects that fall outside of this strategy.
   e. Any changes to the strategy require board approval.
3. Maintain a financially sound organization.
   a. Establish an annual expense budget and an annual fundraising budget.
   b. Ask the Treasurer to present the actual vs. budget (both expenses and fundraising) at every meeting, or at least quarterly.
   c. Make sure the entire board understands and votes to approve and accept these reports at each meeting.
   d. Create financial policies for the organization (cash handling, rainy-day funds, and investments) and be sure they are followed.
   e. Hire an outside auditor annually. Make sure the entire board understands the audit findings and follow-up actions.
4. Approve all policies and be sure they are being followed.
   a. These minimum policies are in place: Conflict of Interest, Ethics Policy, Values Statements.

    b. These organizational policies need to be approved by the entire board: Financial Policies, Human Resource Policies, Donor Policies, Operations Policies.

5. Inspire and manage the Executive Director.

    a. Setup annual objectives and accomplishments for the Executive Director.

    b. Make sure the Chair of the Board provides a written and verbal review for the Executive Director annually.

    c. Insist on training and development for the Executive Director (and all staff members) each year.

    d. Discuss the career path of the *Executive Director each year – make sure they are on track.

6. Create board sustainability.

    a. Create meaningful committees that works closely with the staff and provide both oversight (governance) and organizational support.

    b. For each board committee, create a brief, annual action plan for the work that will be achieved by that committee.

    c. Know what skills are required on your board.

    d. Create an annual system of recruitment and orientation that replaces the skills of the board members whose terms are expiring at the end of each year.

    e. Conduct a board self-evaluation annually.

    f. Create a strong, supportive team that enjoys working together.

If board meetings are not currently focused on the decisions required to govern properly, the board should change that policy immediately. Not only is the board legally responsible to address these key areas of an organization, but leaders of nonprofit organizations should focus their time and attention on the 6 key issues mentioned above.

THE DUTY OF BOARD MEMBERS TO
OVERSEE FINANCIAL OPERATIONS

When a new nonprofit is established, the creator or founders usually recruit a small group of people they know and trust to get things started. These individuals frequently wear many hats, such as bookkeeper, fundraiser, grant writer, and board member.

As the organization grows, the differences between serving on the Board of Directors and volunteering in the program or office become clearer, though many people will continue to serve in multiple roles.

The Board usually has 3-7, maximum 15, members at a time, and most discussions and decisions are made by the group as a whole, especially regarding long-term strategic goals. The Executive Director is generally the decision maker for the day-to-day activities. The Board will eventually understand that in order to maximize the organization's influence, it must expand its efforts beyond its initial program efforts. This usually entails a greater focus on fund raising, financial management, marketing, and evaluation (proving that the organization is good at what it does).

For many organizations, this is the time to start considering bringing on board people with abilities that complement the founding group and figuring out how to set up a good committee structure.

Board committees can provide assistance to employees with critical responsibilities or even handle the work until funds are available for a full-time employee in a small organization.

When committees function, they're fantastic; but when they don't, they're a nightmare. My perspective on committees has evolved over time, and I'd want to share four crucial points:

1. Committees should be developed in response to the organization's present needs, not based on a generic recommendation that "every board should have X, Y, and Z committees."

   It's all too usual for a well-intentioned board member to establish a board structure for an organization based on a generic recommendation or a board member experience with another organization. While most organizations have many committees in common, an organization's first committee experience can be stressful if they try to catch up with a mature organization too early.

   It is recommended that an organization starts with their mission and strategic plan.

   - What tasks must be completed?
   - Over the next one to two years, where will you be concentrating the majority of your efforts?
   - Where can the board's efforts help the organization the most?

Externally focused committees, such as marketing, public relations, and fund raising; and internally focused committees, such as finance and formulating board policies, are common starting points. This assumes that the board officers are already serving as an informal Executive Committee, evaluating and reviewing Executive Directors and providing orientation to incoming board members. Using this method, each committee can determine what additional members and talents it requires, then collaborate with the other board members to find and attract those individuals.

The next committee is usually in charge of evaluating the program or preparing and evaluating it. This group assists in defining "success" for the organization and determining how well you are performing.

2. Except in the case of an all-volunteer organization, committees should complement rather than duplicate staff duties and responsibilities.

   Committees may take on the role of staff members in very small organizations – either temporarily until a staff person is hired or permanently if the organization expects to remain small. In this instance, committee responsibility descriptions may resemble those of staff members.

   However, in most organizations, the board committees serve to assist the board, staff, and the organization in becoming more effective, to relieve them from performing the task themselves.

Board committee members can contribute impartiality to service delivery evaluations and the formulation of external communications. They can also help the organization connect with individuals, firms, and resources that aren't directly accessible to employees.

For instance, the Program Committee or Program Evaluation Committee should concentrate on answering questions such as "What are we aiming to achieve?" and "Are our programs having the desired impact?" The Finance Committee is responsible for ensuring that internal controls are in place to decrease the risk of fraud or theft, as well as recognizing the organization's risks and ensuring that proper insurance and loss prevention plans are in place. In addition, this committee will be responsible for budgets, financial statements, audits, and the form 990 oversight.

Typically, the committees work with a staff person to design a plan before deciding who will carry out the strategy. In a small or no-staff organization, committee members become the key implementers. Committee members serve essential roles in monitoring progress, contributing special knowledge, and developing connections with people, funders, other nonprofit organizations, businesses, or government that can assist the organization in reaching its goals, alongside the organization's personnel.

3. Often board members aren't genuinely engaged until they are responsible for something outside of the regular board sessions.

    When recruiting, nonprofit organizations often tell potential board members that they don't demand much of their time, and then they become unhappy if the board member does do more than the bare minimum. This is a sad reality of board service.
    It can be difficult to get board members to think about the organization for more than 6-8 hours a year if the board meets quarterly (when they are sitting in board meetings). And when an organization meets monthly, it can be difficult to maintain attendance because so little happens in the 30 days between meetings.
    It is easier to establish ties among board members, boost buy-in to the organization, and get more done if they can be involved in a committee that does work that they find interesting and valuable, and that allows them to use their abilities in ways they love.

4. Task Forces (short-term committees) generate energy and focus on achieving a specific goal. Creating standing committees with ill-defined functions can irritate board members and waste their time.
    Treating committees like short-term task forces with a specific mission to fulfill is an effective method to get them started. A Marketing/PR committee, for example, might begin by

organizing a new event or distributing a regular newsletter. Initiatives such as creating a three-year marketing plan" will not generate very much enthusiasm because it is difficult to envision the long-term plan.

Following the initial success, the committees will be able to more readily define the additional abilities and individuals it requires on the team, as well as who the natural leader is. Some committees may be able to function well on a task-by-task basis on a regular basis. Others, such as finance, define their meetings and timetables as more of a regular pattern.

FUNDAMENTALS OF A BOARD
DEVELOPMENT COMMITTEE

Many nonprofit boards prefer to delegate their fundraising responsibilities to the executive director or staff, which happens more frequently than we'd like to think. Successful boards of directors, on the other hand, recognize that they have a critical role to play in ensuring that their organization has the financial resources it requires to operate.

There are certain important considerations for small nonprofits intending to form a fundraising or development committee of the board of directors. Review the tasks that should be part of their role as it relates to fundraising for any organization that may be struggling with an existing board that is not living up to its commitments.

The fundraising and development operations within the organization should be overseen by an effective board development committee. They are in charge of ensuring that the annual fundraising plan is carried out and assessing the progress toward those goals and objectives. They are also in charge of collaborating closely with the development team to assist in finding and obtaining financing from outside sources.

Make no mistake, when your organization approaches major contributors or seeks large gifts from companies or foundations, these potential funders want to meet with leadership, which includes board members.

The development committee's responsibilities are as follows:

- Develop the yearly fundraising targets for the year in collaboration with the Executive Director and fundraising chair.

- Ensure that all on the board of directors understand and approve the overall fundraising goal and development plan.

- Collaborate with the Executive Director and marketing team on the development of the organization's marketing and promotional materials.

- Collaborate with the organization's leadership team to identify individuals, corporations, and foundations for cultivation and solicitation, utilizing all board members' spheres of influence.

- Meet on a regular basis to consider ways to help other members of the board of directors, in addition to the development committee, engage in fundraising activities.

- Collaborate with the Executive Director and fundraising chair to design cultivation, solicitation, and stewardship initiatives for board members' prospects.

- Cultivate, solicit, and steward individuals, corporations, foundations, and companies in partnership with organizational leadership.

- Evaluate the overall non-fundraising profit's efforts in reference to the fundraising plan on a regular basis and make any revisions.

- Assist all board members in achieving any individual and/or aggregate board goals by actively participating in fundraising and aiding all fellow board members in achieving any individual and/or aggregate board objectives.

The board's development committee should be seen as a vital body within the organization's overall board since it assists the nonprofit in obtaining the financial resources it needs to execute its objective.

There is a lot of discussion regarding the board of directors giving and fundraising in the industry. There can be passionate debates about whether or not nonprofit boards should have minimum membership requirements. To put it another way, make it a policy that any board member who serves on a specific board is responsible for raising a specific amount of money.

Whatever approach your organization takes, the ultimate truth is that if there are no board giving minimums, 100 percent board giving should be the minimum.

Board members should be aware that they have a unique responsibility to the organization, one of which is to ensure the nonprofit's budgetary soundness and long-term viability. Having a strong board of directors is one of the best ways to ensure that a nonprofit's fundraising endeavor is successful.

Board members donate their funds, and collect funds from other donors for the smooth functioning of the organization. They utilize all of their resources and funds for achieving overall objectives of organization.

ROLES AND RESPONSIBILITIES OF NONPROFIT FINANCE COMMITTEE

The finance committee is a standing committee of the board of directors and is typically chaired by the board treasurer. The committee is in charge of reviewing and advising on the organization's financial concerns. The committee ensures the organization's internal controls, independent audit, financial analysis, financial transactions, Form 990, and budget are complete and accurate.

The finance committee examines all financial statements and provides updates to the entire board on financial activity. All of the board of directors may be = able to respond better to aggregated data with key financial trends and issues highlighted in a narrative report. While each board member should have the chance to analyze organization-wide revenue and expenditures reports to understand the impact on the organization, unskilled financial statement readers may become lost in overly complex statements. The Executive Director and the finance committee must deliver the facts to the board in a clear and concise way to assist the board in fulfilling its oversight duty.

The finance committee's basic responsibilities are as follows:

1. Set the standard for the remainder of the board in terms of fiscal responsibility.

2. Examine the organization's Statement of Activities, Statement of Financial Position, investments, and other financial matters on a regular basis to insure its long-term viability.

3. Approve the yearly budget and submit it for approval to all of the board of directors.

4. Ensure that a suitable capital structure is maintained.

5. Oversee the upkeep of the organization's assets, including the cautious management of its investments.

The Finance Committee may be asked to perform the following tasks:

1. At a monthly Committee meeting, review revenues and expenses.

2. Ensure that money allocated to the organization is spent wisely (i.e., restricted funds).

3. Create an investment plan.

4. Ensure the annual audit, budget, Form 990, and audited financial statements are completed.

5. Assist employees as necessary.

The finance committee should consist of qualified people who are able to provide the board with essential financial guidance.

THE FINANCE COMMITEE OBLIGATION

The finance committee's primary responsibility is to oversee the organization's finances. Budgeting and financial planning, financial reporting, and the design and monitoring of internal controls and accountability rules are all responsibilities under this committee. The following is a list of responsibilities.

Financial Planning and Budgeting

- With the help of the personnel, create an annual operational budget.
- Within the finance committee, approve the budget. Keep track of how well the budget is being followed by reviewing the actual vs budgeted reports regularly.
- Set long-term financial objectives and funding plans to meet them.
- Create multi-year operating budgets that take into account the strategic plan's goals and ambitions.
- All financial goals and plans should be presented to the board of directors for approval.

In cooperation with the staff administrative head and senior staff, effective finance committees actively participate in an annualized budgeting process. It may be beneficial to include non-board individuals with financial experience, such as a CPA, on the committee unless the organization's bylaws clearly prohibit it.

The committee should identify long-term financial goals in addition to setting an annual budget. These objectives could include the establishment of a working capital or cash reserve fund, as well as the establishment of a fund for the maintenance or replacement of equipment. If the organization has a strategic plan, the finance committee will work with the staff to assess the plan's financial consequences and put them into a multi-year organizational budget that will fund the strategies' implementation.

Creating Financial Reports

With the help of the board members, create report formats that are both useful and readable.

Work with board members to create a list of desired reports, noting the level of detail, frequency, deadlines, and recipients.

Work with board members to understand the reports' consequences. Present the financial reports to all of the board of directors.

If there is an in-house or outsourced bookkeeper or accountant, ensure that they prepare highly detailed reports to the finance committee that clearly communicate the organization's financial and cash condition, adherence to the budget, resource allocation toward the execution of its goal, and support for any donor-imposed contribution restrictions. Your in-house or outsourced bookkeeper or accountant can plan ahead of time to create accurate, high-quality reports and avoid being caught off guard by ad hoc demands if they have a set of reporting expectations.

Furthermore, these reports should help the board's discussion of projected outcomes and appropriate methods for dealing with setbacks or changes in the financial climate, and plan strategically for the future.

Internal Controls and Policies of Accountability

Create, approve, and update (as needed) policies to ensure the organization's assets are protected.

Ensure that financial transaction regulations and procedures are documented in a manual, which is reviewed annually and updated as needed.

Ensure that the financial policies and procedures that have been approved are being followed.

Although the entire board is responsible for the organization's fiduciary responsibility, the finance committee takes the lead in this area, ensuring that suitable internal control processes for all financial transactions are documented in a manual and implemented by employees and board members. The committee should also be responsible for identifying and updating bank account signatories, as well as ensuring that all legal and governmental filing deadlines are satisfied.

Finance committees are frequently tasked with maintaining compliance and/or adopting other policies that help the organization protect itself and manage its risk exposure. This includes setting policies in the areas of:

Personnel guidelines

- Packages of compensation for executives (in the absence of a separate human resources committee)
- Contracts or leases that are for a long period of time
- Lines of credit or loans
- Use of the internet and computer security
- Acceptance of a gift
- Purchases of capital retention of records
- Audits
- Investments
- Donated stock disposition
- Reviewing and requiring insurance

The finance committee may be asked to handle the functions of two other committees that are generally separate in larger organizations – the audit committee and the investment committee – depending on a variety of criteria, such as the size of the board, the size of the budget, and the volume and complexity of existing financial assets.

The following are the basic responsibilities of the audit and investment committees:

Committee of Auditors

- Identify and hire an auditor.
- Examine the draft audit and Form 990 that the auditor has provided.
- The audit report should be presented to the entire board of directors (if the auditor does not do this).
- Examine the auditor's management recommendation letter (SAS112) and verify that any issues raised are followed up on.

Committee on Investments

Prepare an investment policy that outlines the investment portfolio's objectives, asset allocation rules based on a specified level of risk tolerance, authorizations for performing transactions, and the disposition of generated revenue, among other things.

- Ensure that the policy's terms are followed.
- At least once a year, review the policy and, if required, revise it.
- The investment managers/advisors should be hired and evaluated.

Even if a company lacks sufficient cash to fund a full investment portfolio, it should manage its capital to maximize earned revenue. If an organization has excess operating cash, the finance committee, with input from the staff administrative leader, may consider creating guidelines for investing it in low-risk, short-term investment vehicles. Purchase short-term CDs with staggered maturity dates, or set up a sweep account arrangement where surplus cash is swept into a higher-yield vehicle each night to optimize earned revenue from current cash without interfering with operating cash flow demands.

The Finance Committee Chair's Function

The most common chair of the finance committee is the board treasurer, whose specific responsibilities are usually outlined in the organization's bylaws. In practice, these responsibilities might range from a hands-on role, as in the "working board" model, to a more supervisory function, with most transactions handled by employees.

The board treasurer, as chair of the finance committee, ensures that the committee accomplishes its duty. The chair's specific responsibilities include:

- Positioned as the committee's main point of contact with the remainder of the board.

- Creating an agenda for each committee meeting with the help of the staff leader.

- Notifying members of the upcoming meeting.

- Assuring that handouts and reports are produced ahead of time and given to committee members.

- Reviewing the financial statements in board meetings and ask questions that arise or research the required answer.

A yearly committee list is a good way to keep track of the committee's activities. This could be in the form of a month-by-month timetable or calendar that includes budgeting and financial planning deadlines, governmental and legal filing deadlines, internal report deadlines, dates to review and amend policies and procedures, and finance committee and full board meeting dates.

The treasurer or finance committee chair does not have to be a professional "numbers" person, but must have sound judgement, rationality, curiosity, and a dedication to accountability and the organization's long-term financial stability. A good treasurer or finance committee chair will understand nonprofit financial reporting and the IRS Form 990, or will quickly learn to do so.

A fully engaged finance committee is a significant indication that an organization is committed to good stewardship and is actively building and protecting the financial resources required to support the execution of its purpose in the short and long term.

IRS RULES CONCERNING DONATIONS

The IRS allows individuals and businesses to make noncash contributions to qualifying charities and to claim deductions for these contributions on their tax returns. Gifts of donated property, clothing, and other noncash items have long been an important source of revenue for many charitable organizations and a popular deduction for taxpayers.

Charitable gifts made to most nonprofit organizations that are officially recognized by the IRS as having 501(c) (3) status are considered to be tax deductible contributions. Such donations are contributions of money or goods to a tax-exempt organization. These tax-deductible donations can reduce the donor's taxable income.

Issuance of tax-compliant donation receipt

Donations by an individual or corporation making the donation to a 501(c)(3) organization are tax-deductible. However, before the donations can be claimed as tax deductions, a donation receipt needs to be issued by the nonprofit organization to the donor.

A donation receipt is a written acknowledgment issued by a nonprofit to the donor who made a contribution to the organization. This will be the official proof to the IRS that the donor made a donation to the nonprofit organization.

Without the receipt, donors will not be able to claim any tax deduction. The donors may request the donor letter so that they will be able to claim the donations on their tax returns. The donation letter should be:

- A written communication from the nonprofit for any contribution in terms of cash.
- A written acknowledgment from the organization for a single contribution of $250 or more.
- A written disclosure for donors who received goods or services in exchange for a single payment above $75.

The following items must be included on the receipt for the donors to successfully claim a tax deduction:

- The name of your organization.
- The amount of the cash contribution received.
- A description of the non-cash contribution (value is not required).
- If no goods or services were provided, a statement that says so.
- If goods or services were provided, a description of the goods and services offered and a fair value estimate of those goods and services.
- For nonprofits that are operating exclusively for religious purposes, a statement that such goods or services provided in return for contribution are intangible religious benefits, i.e., not commercial transactions.

- Donor's name.

- The date when the contribution is received.

Including the nonprofit organization's address and Employer Identification Number (EIN) is great, but this is not a must, according to IRS.

Note: An organization must already have obtained the tax-exempt status through the IRS so donors can claim the contributions as tax-deductible. Therefore, it is important that nonprofit organization's keeps track of its tax-exempt status and ensures that it stays up to date with IRS notifications.

A popular fundraising solution is the sale of donated property. Nonprofits may also use donated property in their tax-exempt programs.

Quid Pro Quo Contributions

This type of contribution is a payment a donor makes to a charity partly as a contribution and partly for goods or services. For example, if a donor gives a charity $100 and receives a concert ticket valued at $40, the donor has made a quid pro quo contribution. In this example, the charitable contribution part of the payment is $60. Even though the deductible part of the payment is not more than $75, a disclosure statement must be provided by the organization to the donor because the donor's payment (quid pro quo contribution) is more than $75. Failure to make the required disclosure may result in a penalty to the organization.

Disclosure Statement

The required written disclosure statement must:

a. Inform the donor that the amount of the contribution that is deductible for federal income tax purposes is limited to the excess of any money (and the value of any property other than money) contributed by the donor over the fair market value of goods or services provided by the charity, and

b. Provide the donor with a good faith estimate of the fair market value of the goods or services that the donor received. The nonprofit must furnish the statement in connection with either the solicitation or the receipt of the quid pro quo contribution. If the disclosure statement is furnished in connection with a particular solicitation, it is not necessary for the organization to provide another statement when it actually receives the contribution.

No disclosure statement is required if any of the following is true:

i. The goods or services given to a donor have insubstantial value.

ii. There is no donative element involved in a particular transaction with a nonprofit (for example, there is generally no donative element involved in a visitor's purchase from a museum gift shop).

iii. There is only an intangible religious benefit provided to the donor. The intangible religious benefit must be provided to the donor by an organization organized exclusively for religious purposes, and must be of a type that generally is not sold in a commercial transaction outside the donative context. For example, a donor who, for a payment, is granted admission to a religious ceremony for which there is no admission charge is provided an intangible religious benefit. However, a donor is not provided intangible religious benefits for payments made for tuition for education leading to a recognized degree, travel services, or consumer goods.

iv.   The donor makes a payment of $75 or less per year and receives only annual membership benefits that consist of:

1. Any rights or privileges (other than the right to purchase tickets for college athletic events) that the taxpayer can exercise often during the membership period, such as free or discounted admissions or parking or preferred access to goods or services, or

2. Admission to events that are open only to members and the cost per person of which is within the limits for low-cost or insubstantial value.

Good Faith Estimates of Fair Market Value

An organization may use any reasonable method to estimate the fair market value (FMV) of goods or services it provided to a donor, as long as it applies the method in good faith. The organization may estimate the FMV of goods or services that generally are not commercially available by using the FMV of similar or comparable goods or services. Goods or services may be similar or comparable even if they do not have the unique qualities of the goods or services being valued.

Example 1. A nonprofit provides a one-hour golf lesson with a golf professional for the first $500 payment received. The golf professional provides one-hour lessons on a commercial basis for $200. A good faith estimate of the lesson's FMV is $200.

Example 2. For a payment of $50,000, a museum allows a donor to hold a private event in a room of the museum. A good-faith estimate of the FMV of the right to hold the event in the museum can be made by using the cost of renting a hotel ballroom with a capacity, amenities, and atmosphere comparable to the museum room, even though the hotel ballroom lacks the unique art displayed in the museum room. If the hotel ballroom rents for $2,500, a good faith estimate of the FMV of the right to hold the event in the museum is $2,500.

Example 3. For a payment of $1,000, a nonprofit provides an evening tour of a museum conducted by a well-known artist. The artist does not provide tours on a commercial basis. Tours of the museum normally are free to the public. A good faith estimate of the FMV of the evening museum tour is $0 even though the artist conducts it.

Penalty for Failure to Disclose

A penalty is imposed on a charity that does not make the required disclosure of a quid pro quo contribution of more than $75. The penalty is $10 per contribution, not to exceed $5,000 per fundraising event or mailing. The charity can avoid the penalty if it can show that the failure was due to reasonable cause.

IN-KIND DONATIONS AND FINANCIAL STATEMENTS

If a nonprofit organization accepts in-kind donations, it is important that they are recorded and reported in a systematic fashion.

To assist in understanding the dynamics of such a task, this section will explain how in-kind donations work as well as the methods by which nonprofit organizations can classify and report them on the financial statements.

While not intended as a comprehensive resource, this general overview will help to understand the benefits of an organized process for tracking and recording these donations, as well as, how they can be useful for internal management teams.

Recording In-Kind Gifts

In general, any nonprofit organization that prepares its financial statements in accordance with Generally Accepted Accounting Principles (GAAP) must record and report all in-kind donations.

Nonprofits that undergo annual auditing by an independent firm must also adhere to this standard, sometimes as required by law or as stipulated through stakeholder agreement, lending agent, grantor, or other structural mechanisms.

Tracking of in-kind donations is beneficial for purposes of strategic planning and as an internal audit of operations.

Timing of Recording In-Kind Gifts to Nonprofit Organizations

As a general rule, in-kind donations are recorded upon receipt by the organization. If there is a number of recurring donations, then they are posted within the period they are received. Minimally speaking, donations must be recorded on an annualized basis.

The Valuation Process for In-Kind Donations

The standard process for assigning a value to an in-kind donation received is to use the "fair value" metric.

Fair value defined

"Fair value" basically refers to an item's market price or what a buyer would reasonably pay for the item in question if it were available for sale. This also applies to transactions in which an expense is transferred from one party to another. The fair value would be the cost of transferring that expense from one party to another.

Here are a few examples:

If an organization receives a piece of equipment, the fair value would be what the organization would have to pay to buy that same item on the market. This applies to items the nonprofit can use as well as those it may sell or even donate, such as computers and other office equipment.

If a professional donates their time and energy to a nonprofit organization, the number of hours spent on those tasks should be tracked as well as the market rate cost the nonprofit would pay to obtain those services independently. To determine the market rate of the cost of services, contact the donor and ask them to place a value on the in-kind services.

For items that are difficult to ascertain in value, asking the donor to assign a value to the item is also possible.

Acknowledgment of In-Kind Donations: Formally and Informally

Aside from a thank-you note or other letter from your organization to the donor to thank them for their gift, also provide them with documentation recording the gift, the date received, the amount, and the person who gifted it for both organizational and the donor's tax purposes.

Following the IRS guidelines, organizations must provide donors with a written acknowledgment of receipt of the item or service before that donor can claim the deduction for tax purposes. Further, this acknowledgment of receipt must be sent for any donation totaling $250 or more.

The Format of the Acknowledgment

When sending acknowledgments to donors, it is beneficial to both the recipient and the organization for donation letters to be presented in a systematic fashion. Not only does this help with bookkeeping and filing down the road, but also it brings clarity to the process that makes auditing and strategic planning much easier.

First, the nonprofit should designate an officer as the official person to send out all gift acknowledgments. This can be the board of directors' chair, board of directors' treasurer, Executive Director, or other management.

Generally, organizations should aim to send out acknowledgments within 30 days of receipt of the donation in question.

Making sure that organizations receive such documentation in a timely fashion is important for several reasons, but, most importantly, it helps the donor prepare financial statements and taxes.

Elements to include in donation letters

The IRS provides very clear guidance on what tax-exempt organizations should put in the acknowledgment letter.

Fundamentals of the letter include restating the organization's tax-exempt status, the date of the donation, a description of the item with a value assigned, and a statement from the nonprofit that it did not exchange any goods or services to receive the donation.

If the donation was greater than $75 and the nonprofit did exchange goods or services, then the nonprofit must detail a fair estimated value of those goods and services.

Tracking Donations and Acknowledgments

To make the process of tracking donations and their corresponding acknowledgments easier on an organization, it is recommended that they maintain a database or utilize a customer relationship management (CRM) system.

These CRMs are increasingly sophisticated in terms of their ability to automate tasks and tackle a great deal of the grunt work associated with the recording and tracking of in-kind donations to nonprofit organizations. They also assist with strategic planning and can even be operationalized to administer and maintain marketing campaigns and outreach efforts.

The accepted way to record in-kind donations is to set up a separate revenue account but the expense side of the transaction should be recorded in its functional expense account. For example, revenue would be recorded as Gifts In-Kind – Goods, and the expense would be recorded as Goods given. Once you've determined the fair value of your donation, you'll record the journal entry. The in-kind revenue will equal the in-kind expense. These transactions will not have any net impact on your financials, but it will impact your organization's total revenue and expenses, and it is a requirement of both FASB and the IRS.

PAYING THE STAFF

Many nonprofit organizations generally use volunteers to carry out their mission. However, a nonprofit is also a business and must have qualified paid staff that is committed to operating and maintaining the organization and delivering effective services. The organization's paid staff is essential to operations and helping the organization reach its mission.

Both state law, which governs nonprofits, and the IRS, which regulates the tax-exempt status, allows nonprofit organizations to pay reasonable salaries to officers, employees, or agents for services provided to further the organization's mission.

There aren't rules that exist for compensation in a nonprofit, but the IRS can penalize both an organization and an individual for excessive pay. This is exemplified in the inurement clause governing nonprofit organizations. The inurement clause states that the resources of the nonprofit must not benefit a private party. Excess pay would violate this obligation.

Overpaying a staff member may cause the nonprofit organization to pay an excise tax and it could lose its tax-exempt status. With the 2018 tax law change, nonprofits that pay high compensation will pay an excise tax (penalty) of 21% on compensation over $1 million dollars on the top 5 highest-paid employees.

Knowing the market rate when hiring new staff members is helpful and can be found by reviewing comparability data. This includes salary and benefits information from other nonprofits in the same or similar geographical area with a similar budget and mission focus.

Payroll tax liability

Although most nonprofits are tax-exempt, the IRS still requires them to pay payroll taxes. An organization must pay the appropriate employment taxes for employees, such as Social Security, FICA, and state and federal income taxes. Failure to pay these taxes will lead to large fines.

Furthermore, any "responsible person" can be held personally liable if payroll taxes are not timely paid. This means the person must pay the back taxes and penalties out of his/her own pocket. A responsible person may include not only a nonprofit's accountant or bookkeeper, but anyone who exercises significant control over the nonprofit's finances. This can include not only a nonprofit's treasurer, president, executive director, CEO, and other officers, but its board members as well.

Even if an individual is not directly involved in paying payroll taxes, liability can be found. In one case, the chairman of the board of directors of a nonprofit was held personally liable for nonpayment of payroll taxes. Even though the organization's Executive Director and bookkeeper were the ones who were responsible, according their job descriptions outlined by the board, for ensuring the taxes were paid.

Employees or Independent Contractors

Nonprofits should pay close attention to their labor costs. Employees should be hired to fill key positions, and use independent contractors to assist with time-bound projects, busy periods, planned and unplanned absences, and specialty needs (e.g., accounting and grant writing). Using contractors will save money the organization would spend on payroll taxes, payroll administration, workers compensation insurance, and employee benefits.

It also offers organizations the ability to align labor costs with estimated funding, tasks, and projects for the fiscal year. It also provides flexibility in managing expenses when actual funding falls short of anticipation.

However, misclassifying employees could expose a nonprofit organization to significant financial and business risk. If contractors who should be classified as employee file a law suit, governmental agencies could assess fines and penalties. In addition, federal and state grants could be at risk. And potential insurers could deny access to coverage.

According to the IRS, if an organization tells an employee what to do, when to do it, and how to do it, generally they would be classified as an employee. This includes what work the individual must do (versus delegate to others), what tools or equipment to use, what order to follow, where and how to purchase supplies and services, and where to perform the work.

When it comes to independent contractors, an employer can specify the desired outcome for the work but not the method of performing services.

Independent contractors generally invest in the tools they use to perform work (e.g., computers, software, office equipment, etc.) and they are not reimbursed by clients. They typically provide their services to other organizations. And they usually are paid a flat-rate or time-and-materials basis instead of receiving a specific wage. There are many good business reasons to classify a worker as an independent contractor, and many situations when that classification is appropriate.

Note: If the laborer provides services that are essential to the operation of the organization, then it increases the chances that the organization controls that individual's work performance. Careful analysis and due diligence in partnership with a professional tax advisor are a good investment of time and money to protect your business from potential liability.

Board Members Compensation

Can nonprofit board members be compensated by the organizations they serve? The answer is "Maybe." There are a few limitations.

The board members are a group of volunteers that is officially involved in the governance of a nonprofit. Due to concerns regarding conflicts of interest, a clear distinction is required between paid employees and volunteers for a nonprofit organization.

Legal implications with paying board members

There is no federal law prohibiting nonprofit board members from being compensated, and the vast majority of nonprofit board members are unpaid. They may, however, be compensated for specific costs or claim a tax deduction on their own income taxes.

Your organization's regulations may, however, prevent any compensation except for repayment of expenses or services given by the board members. The organization's conflict-of-interest policy may also have an impact on board member compensation.

It should be noted that appropriate pay for board member services is permitted with safeguards and if the organization's bylaws allow it. For instance, ensuring that the pay is fair and comparable to what a similar-sized nonprofit provides. If a board member's annual pay exceeds $600, your organization must file Form 1099 Misc to the IRS unless they are classified as an employee. In that case, they will receive a Form W-2.

Paying the Executive Director

The board of directors is responsible for hiring, and establishing compensation, both salary and benefits, of the Executive Director or CEO by identifying compensation that is reasonable and not excessive. The recommended steps for determining the appropriate compensation are to research the market to determine what similar size organizations, in the same geographic region, offer their senior leaders.

Nonprofits filing Form 990 must explain the process used to approve the Executive Director's compensation on the annual return.

Paying board members

A paid board member is obviously conflicted since he or she has a clear self-interest in getting paid, no matter how big or small the paycheck is. The IRS is often concerned about such conflicts because it needs to ensure that private persons do not improperly collect charitable assets that should instead be used for the public good.

Nonprofits typically do not compensate board members since their mission is to serve the public and not to benefit any one or group of persons. Paying board members may also create a conflict of interest and undermine the financial integrity of a nonprofit. Paid board members may also potentially lose their immunity from litigation brought against the organization.

This is because a volunteer board member often has substantial legal protection against personal responsibility originating from the nonprofit's operations, such as defamation, auto accidents, slip-and-fall accidents, trademark infringement, and so on.

There may be certain exceptions, but they are usually restricted to the board member's own "gross negligence," often known as "wanton misconduct," deliberate misconduct, or liability under other statutory schemes. An example of this is the personal liability arising from knowingly misusing employment taxes.

When a board member starts getting paid, the legal hurdle will be lowered, and the board member may face responsibility based on a judgment of "ordinary negligence." Whether it is gross negligence or ordinary negligence and whether it is enough to warrant for personal liability depend solely upon the jury, whose verdicts are known to be notoriously unpredictable.

Typically, it will not be difficult to find community leaders to serve as volunteer board members. The benefits for those board members include the ability to give back to the community that they serve, meet other prominent individuals in their community, improve their professional reputations, and learn about community needs.

Paying nonprofits' board members may be great and totally reasonable. If your nonprofit decides to do so, be sure to have a conflict-of-interest policy in place. This policy should be applied when having independent and careful board discussions. Based on this policy, all compensated Executive Directors must be treated as salaried employees.

You should also check the board members' insurance plans. The board members' insurance plans may give certain legal protection, particularly if compensation is a major priority. This differential legal standard for personal liability may be worth careful consideration for your organization if it decides to pay the board members minor wages or rewards for their board participation.

Determining board members pay

As a result, if a board member is to be compensated, he or she should withdraw from the relevant board meetings to determine compensation, to prevent conflict. Any other related and affected board member also should be excused, such as the spouse, other family members, or business associates of the member to be compensated.

The ideal situation would be for at least two independent, non-conflicted directors to evaluate if the member is the best candidate for the job and if the proposed compensation level is reasonable and in the best interests of the organization.

Members of the board who participate in such a decision-making process must uphold their fiduciary responsibilities of due diligence and duty of care. Other possible job applicants may also be evaluated as part of the due diligence process.

Furthermore, compensation levels for similar roles should be compared, taking into account their skills, experience, and education. Your organization can use www.guidestar.org as a guideline. This website has made nonprofit organizations' Form 990s and executive directors' salary data (those that are submitted via Form 990) available to the general public.

GuideStar shares nonprofit reports and Forms 990 for donors, grant makers, and businesses. GuideStar connects donors and grant makers to non-profit organizations.

Board of director's reimbursement

Despite the fact that board members are not normally paid, they may be compensated for expenses such as those incurred to travel to a board meeting in another city or to attend a conference. Board members may be able to deduct uncompensated expenses if they are not reimbursed.

Nonprofits are allowed to repay nonprofit board members for expenditures incurred while serving the organization; such expenditures include travel or donor-related fees. It does not count as compensation, but instead as reimbursement for justifiable nonprofit expense.

Some nonprofits may ask their board members to pay for these expenditures out of their own pockets as a matter of organizational policy, although this is not required by law. However, if the organization confirms the amount with an official receipt, the board members may be allowed to claim it as a tax-deductible cost.

REASONABLE COMPENSATION
DEFINED

The IRS recommends that nonprofit organizations follow a three-step process to determine if compensation is reasonable and not excessive.

1. The board should arrange for an "independent body." This means that the person receiving the compensation should not be a part of the review process to conduct a comparability review.

2. The independent body should take a look at "comparable" salary and benefits data, such as data available from salary and benefits surveys, to learn what nonprofit employers with similar missions, and similar budget size, that are located in the same or similar geographic region, pay their senior leaders.

3. The board/independent body that is conducting the review should document who was involved, their independence (i.e., they do not receive compensation from the nonprofit) and the process used to conduct the review, as well as the disposition of the full board's decision to approve the executive director's compensation. This information should be included in the meeting minutes. The documentation should demonstrate that the board took the comparable data into consideration when it approved compensation.

TRAINING NONPROFIT BOARD MEMBERS TO READ AND UNDERSTAND FINANCIAL REPORTS

One of the responsibilities of board members is to keep a record of the organization's financial situation. As a result, board members should be familiar with the financial reports that the organization utilizes to illustrate its financial health. The variety of financial reports typically used by most nonprofits are identified in this book to emphasize the importance of training board members to read and understand financial reports.

The following are some examples of common financial reports:

1. Statement of Activities, similar to the Income Statement – this financial statement summarizes all of the revenue and expenses for a given period of time. It is used to categorize the different revenue sources and expenses. The revenue portion is usually first, followed by the expense section. The net assets are calculated by subtracting total expenditure from total revenue. Losses are usually denoted by a negative sign (-) before the actual figure. The goal of this report is to reflect the financial situation of the organization over the specified time period.

Plus, you can use this document to review the change in net assets from the beginning of the year to the end of the year.

The Statement of Activities in nonprofit accounting can be summarized by this simple equation:

Revenue – Expenses = Net Assets

The Statement of Activities is normally reviewed by board members monthly or quarterly, generally during their board meeting.

2. Statement of Financial Position, similar to the Balance Sheet, represents the financial health of your organization the most. This report itemizes the organization's assets and liabilities and offers a picture of the organization's financial situation at a given point in time, rather than across a period of time.

   The statement of financial position in nonprofit accounting can be summarized by this simple equation:

Net Assets = Assets - Liabilities

By understanding how these sections work together, the board will be able to better understand the general financial health of your organization by reviewing this report. Positive net assets indicate healthier financials at your organization while negative net assets mean you need to make some financial changes. At least once a month or quarter, board members should analyze the organization's balance sheet.

3. Statement of Functional Expenses breaks down nonprofit organizations' expenses into various functional categories. The

categories separate expenses into one of three operational functions: program expenses, administrative expenses, or fundraising activity expenses.

The detailed information included on the statement of functional expenses also helps when it's time to complete the annual Form 990, which requires expenses to categorized separately.

4. Cash flow statement – this statement shows the funding inflow and outflow of cash and cash equivalents inside the organization. It allows you to gauge how much is available to pay your expenses at any given time. These statements are helpful in establishing an organization's short-term survival, particularly its capacity to pay its obligations. Examining an organization's cash flow is crucial at any time, but it's especially crucial for new organization or those that have recently suffered financial difficulties.

The nonprofit cashflow statement shows the operating, financing and investing activities to show how cash moves in your organization. This report shows the uses of funding received from fundraising, grant seeking, and other revenue streams by analyzing the statement.

5. Monthly budgeted vs actual report - this report compares the organization's monthly income (what it received) to its monthly expenditures (what it spent), as well as its projected income and expenditures. For example, if an organization budgeted $3,000 for office supplies each year and has already spent the whole budget halfway through the year, the board

should inquire as to why this occurred (e.g., was the money that was initially allotted for this line item insufficient, was the organization not tracking expenses for this line item, did the organization suffer an unanticipated expenditure, etc.).

If the board meets on a monthly basis, it should go over the financial report from the preceding month. If the board meets every other month or quarterly, it should go over any financial reports that have been released since the last meeting.

6. If the organization receives an annual audit of financial statements, the Notes to the Financial Statements will be included. The Notes to Financial Statements are integral part of the nonprofit organization's audited financial statements. It provides a detailed report on the aspects that are necessary users' understanding of the financial statements. It provides disclosures on restrictions, liquidity etc., for the donors, creditors, and other stakeholders.

7. The Form 990 is the annual form that tax-exempt organizations are required to file each year to remain compliant with regulations and requirements set by the IRS. Filing the annual Form 990 is an important part of nonprofit accounting.

In the Form 990, nonprofit revenue and expenses from the year demonstrate how finances have been utilized. Essentially, the Form 990 is the IRS method of evaluating nonprofit organizations' financial honesty and legitimacy.

Board members should be taught to read and understand financial reports. While some board members may be familiar with financial reports, the majority do not understand or know how to analyze financial data. This type of training should be included in new-board-member orientation as well as continuous training. You may have an experienced executive director or board member to provide the training, or you could ask your bookkeeper or accountant to instruct new and present board members. Whatever technique you choose, make sure your board members have the skills to read, comprehend, and monitor financial data.

REASONS ACCOUNTING IS IMPORTANT

Decisions can be made faster. As a board member or the founder of a nonprofit, many of the challenges encountered are time sensitive and require immediate attention. Accounting provides the ability to get up-to-date information on all financial elements of the organization, which can be crucial in making educated decisions in various scenarios.

Nonprofit accounting reports provide decision-makers with key information to understand an organization's financial status, funding streams, and developing strategies. Financial statements include information about balances, revenues, and expenses. It also tracks how money is spent in different funds.

That means that the board or finance committee members may use the reports and share them with others, allowing everyone to make informed choices based on accurate and realistic financial facts.

Reduce likelihood of fraud. It's a terrible truth, but nonprofits are vulnerable to fraud from inside their own organizations or from outside sources. An employee could try to take advantage of internal controls for their personal financial gains.

With accounting, an organization could prevent any possible fraud as it includes simplifying and enhancing internal controls. This will lead to fewer opportunities for someone to exploit the internal systems and engage in criminal behavior.

It will also mean that an audit for an organization will be easier to carry out, saving time and also money.

It keeps the funding flowing. Nonprofit organizations need to ensure all their expenses are documented and fall within the constraints of the organization's nonprofit charter. For example, if an organization is subjected to an audit and it is discovered that the nonprofit did not have a formal accounting process in place and is unable to provide documentation for thousands of dollars spent in expenses, they will not have a clean audit. If an audit encountered problems with documentation, the organization could lose future funding. With so many non-profit organizations operating on tight budgets, it's vital to maintain accounting accuracy.

Attention to detail is required in accounting for a nonprofit organization's transactions. Since some contributions have requirements attached to them focusing on how they are to be used, accounting in a nonprofit organization needs to show stakeholders where the funds have been spent. Failure to provide the necessary information can lead to violations of an organization's tax-exempt status.

ESTABLISHING A BUDGET

Budgeting for nonprofit organizations can be complex because of involvement of several overlapping categories, like functions, grants, programs, and nature. It is also complex because sources of income are not secure at beginning stage of making a budget. Budgets may require modifications. Using accounting software provides the ability to compare actual amounts verses the budgeted amounts.

Creating an efficient and empowering budget is important because so many people are counting on the organization to succeed. The annual budgeting process usually involves estimating the amount of money the organization needs to raise and spend throughout the year. It's a tedious and painstaking process that, if not approached correctly, might throw off annual goals.

A nonprofit's budget and strategic plan should go hand-in-hand. Every aspect of the budget should be directly associated with a specifically defined activity that will be accomplished. In addition, each of these activities should have a specifically defined separate budget. These separate budgets all combine into the singular organization-wide operational budget.

General budgeting rules for nonprofits

A nonprofit operating budget breaks down the annual projected revenue and expenses for the organization. It breaks down the revenue by different funding sources and operating expenses by program and overhead costs.

Throughout the year, the budgets should be reviewed regularly to monitor the process of various projects, fundraising success, and financial standing. This means a budget is a living document that should be at the center of your financial activities.

Organize the financial data.

Nonprofits should follow professional bookkeeping and accounting standards to ensure their budgets are on point. The organization's historical records and financial data are used to make strategic and informed financial decisions.

Estimate the annual income.

Expected revenue should be separated and allocated by each fundraising source. Use past data from the finance team to better understand and predict how much will need to be raised from each source. Analyze the success of past fundraising campaigns and predict the annual income (i.e., fundraising, grants, sponsorship, donations, etc.) accordingly.

Consider fixed expenses first.

Fixed expenses, like office rent, paychecks, utility bills, and other operational costs, should be a major part of your budget. They are also known as administrative expenses. These are predictable expenses that you should prioritize. After all, there are risks associated with payment delays.

Analyze the variable or flexible expenses.

These are not unnecessary expenses. Indeed, these are difficult to plan due to their nature to fluctuate. But you should analyze them from year to year to be better prepared. This could include office supplies, conferences out of town, hiring temporary help for the office or programs, and costs associated with hosting events and fundraisers.

Estimate the Program, Research, and Service Costs.

While some nonprofits focus on conducting research with the goal of finding a treatment or cure for a specific disease, others focus on providing services or programs to help the local community. Program expenses are those that are necessary to conduct your work in the community. These programs may include donations of clothing or food from the public, while others require funding to pay tutors who offer assistance to underprivileged children, for example. These programs cost money to operate and will vary depending on the size and scope.

Fundraising expenses should be projected.

Fundraising expenses can be broken down into marketing campaigns, fundraising advisor, fundraising event venue or virtual software investment, and fundraising technology tools.

Include Professional Services expenses in the budget.

Many nonprofits hesitate to hire a consultant, mostly because of cost. However, what's most important is that you find a nonprofit consultant who's the right fit for your organization: someone who can work well with your team, understand your nonprofit's unique needs, and offer sustainable solutions to your problems. The key is to prioritize, to plan ahead, to anticipate costs and budget, and to frame nonprofit professional fees such that your board and high-level donors understand the importance of these expenses. Nonprofit consultants, such as attorneys, CPAs, accountants, grant writers, and fundraisers can help with long-term initiatives or short-term campaigns.

Conduct annual budget analysis.

By examining what was spent in the past is the best way to estimate a nonprofit's expenses. Best practice is to separate the organizational fixed and variable expenses, then estimate what various budget items will cost. Annual budget analysis helps make better expense predictions and keep the variable expenses in check. We highly recommend outsourcing budget analysis to experts or at least including one in the discussion.

Budgeting tips nonprofits should follow

Now that we have set the ground rules, it's time we start building on them. Here are some of the best budgeting tips for nonprofits.

Establish a timeline.

Getting the budget approved and setting check-ins for the team is imperative. Before starting the budgeting process, the finance committee should set a day and time when the budget will be approved by the board. This holds everyone accountable by providing a due date to complete the plan.

Regular check-ins should be established with the finance committee to ensure the team is staying on track with the timeline and budget planned out. Many nonprofits do a quick check-in monthly with a more in-depth review each quarter.

Set financial goals.

Come up with a detailed and multi-year analysis of what the nonprofit organization wants to achieve. The board should have a clear vision of how to ground the budget. The best way to set financial goals is by creating a budget based on estimates of past data.

Each of the activities should be associated with a specific dollar amount for each expense and revenue source. This is especially important when developing the revenue portion of the budget. A nonprofit's funding should be collected from different sources of revenue streams.

For example, if it is expected that your organization will receive $75,000 from individual fundraising this year, it may be determined that $50,000 will be collected from major donors, $10,000 from your direct mail campaign, $10,000 from the donation page on the website, $5,000 from online fundraising.

These funding metrics should be realistic. Setting the metrics too high and it may discourage the team. Past fundraising successes can assist the finance committee in determining realistic numbers.

Begin with a general template.

Create a budget draft that clearly defines the primary income sources and basic expenses. Consider the basic line items like personnel costs, office costs, and other essential expenses. Create detailed line items to develop a precise and explanatory budget (more on this later).

Have realistic budget line items.

The line items should be realistic and manageable. As we mentioned earlier, more line items can be added to create a detailed budget, but it might make the budget overly complicated. A complex budget limits the flexible allocation of funds. Minimizing the line items helps to avoid complicating the budget. Only include the detailed line items that are significant. Miscellaneous amounts can be combined with similar line items.

Ensure a monthly budgeted vs actual distribution.

The distribution of the budgeted versus actuals monthly allows expenses and activities to be managed on a monthly basis. Why? A monthly budget distribution provides the opportunity to track monthly progress with complete accuracy, which further eases budget realignments. Not just that, monthly budgeted versus actuals also allow breaking down and accounting for the different monthly activities, especially the ones having one-time costs.

Factor in inflation for each line item.

One of the ground rules we discussed earlier was annual budget analysis. A huge part of that is figuring out the inflation of different line items. Check the previous year's records to estimate the inflation. Use the data to account for inflation for the current year. In addition, consider the current market conditions and how they may affect expenses in the future. This is all the more important when creating a multi-year budget.

Account for seasonality.

Nonprofits usually devise a single budget for the year. However, there will be many timing inconsistencies which should be considered while drafting the budget. Account for seasonality and timing of income sources and expenses. Consider the months that more revenue is expected or have more expenses. This allows nonprofits to plan expenses and reserve enough cash for such expenses. For example, if it is known that #GivingTuesday and year-end giving is a major source of revenue for the organization, try to complete a larger project directly after these campaigns.

Document budget decisions.

Lastly, record every decision and assumption made related to the budget. Prepare a consolidated budget spreadsheet and share it with all of the board members to keep them on the same page. Taking note of every decision and assumption gives the opportunity to make better budgets in the coming years.

FINANCIAL OVERSIGHT – WHY NONPROFIT BOARDS NEED TO REVIEW MORE THAN THE OPERATING BUDGET

The difference between the budget and the financial statements: The operating budget is merely a plan to guide in managing the money needed to manage day-to-day operational expenses. The financial statements are reports that represent the organization's true financial status. The budget was created by the board, and it may be changed at any time. The financial reports were prepared in accordance with generally accepted accounting principles and represent the organization's complete financial picture. Financial statements cannot be changed at any time by the board (unless it wants to be open to legal problems).

The board should evaluate both the budget and the major financial reports every month. What is the reason for this? The operating budget simply shows one aspect of the organization, whereas the financial reports provide a comprehensive picture. Because board members are in charge of the nonprofit's financial management, they need to be able to see the full picture in order to accomplish their mission correctly.

The financial statements still contain a budget review, but they also include two critical financial reports, labelled the "Statement of Financial Conditions" and "Statement of Activities."

THE UNIQUENESS OF NONPROFITS ACCOUNTING

Accounting is an important step for any organization. Many individuals believe that accounting is only for profit-focused firms, because profit-focused organizations typically have more financial resources to handle and track. For nonprofits, accounting keeps track of such financial transactions as grants, donations, budgeting, payroll, and other expenses.

Just like a profit-oriented business, a nonprofit organization also needs to record, plan, and report its finances. The purpose of preparing financial statements is to allow the board of directors to stay accountable to the stakeholders, which include the donors, contributors, and members.

With that said, the financial statements of nonprofits are very unique in the way that they focus on accountability instead of profitability. That means the users of a nonprofit organization's financial statements would direct their attention to how the funds are used in the organization when reading the financial statements.

In-house accounting divisions are commonly used by nonprofit organizations to manage accounting tasks. Accounting teams are in charge of producing financial reports and paperwork for the organization. These reports are used by management to evaluate the state of the organization, as well as to identify any financial imbalances or irregularities.

CPAs and other skilled professionals frequently make up accounting teams. These CPAs are in charge of the accounting department's top roles, overseeing all of the team's tasks and obligations. The head CPA engages with the organization's management on a regular basis to update financial reporting. Bookkeeping and auditing, which are both critical accounting operations, may be handled by clerks or assistants on the team.

An organization's accounting requirements might be complex, especially if it conducts large-scale operations. Because nonprofit organizations have more financial information to keep track of, accounting for them may be even more difficult.

Accounting can be difficult for organizations to understand. Nonprofit tax rules are strict, and keeping track of all your fluctuating funding sources can be difficult. Fortunately, you can ensure total compliance and transparency when it comes to your nonprofit organization's financials by using the correct accounting methods. This section assists you in better understanding how nonprofit accounting works and the best ways of its use.

Depending on the organization, usually the donors of these nonprofits have the right to set restrictions on the money they contributed to the organization. Certain grant funders would also require the organization to spend the funds they provided only on specific allowable programs.

Such restrictions would mean that the funds received by the organization need to be closely monitored and approved each time the funds are utilized. To account for this (no pun intended), nonprofits will use fund accounting.

Fund Accounting Defined

Fund accounting is a transparency technique use by nonprofit organizations for all funds and grants received from individuals, grant authorities, governments, or any other associations. It records the resources of nonprofit organizations.

Fund accounting is a type of accounting system. It is mainly used by nonprofits, governments, and government agencies to track accountability rather than profitability.

It helps the organization to make sure that all incomes received are grouped into different fund categories based on their purpose and source. This is especially useful for larger organizations with multiple sources of fund income.

With fund accounting, nonprofits would be able to differentiate clearly between the proceeds received and spend them only for which they are designated.

In this method, funds consist of self-sustaining set of financial records and each of them are stated as unrestricted and restricted depending upon donor's instructions. The donor's limitations are generally associated in writing and through agreement. The organization regulates and documents the funds received from the donors. The overall objectives of fund accounting include:

- Better decision-making regarding use of scarce resources.
- Identifying decisions, goals, and objectives related to the financial management of resources.
- Reporting the information of activities for user's understanding.
- Recording information about sources of donations or income and their use for meeting the intended purposes.

Nonprofit organizations rely directly on many funding entities. Generally, the proceeds can be split into the following main categories:

Some donors limit their donations to certain causes or activities. In financial management, these must be taken into account. Non-donor-restricted funds can be utilized for any program, administrative costs, or other needs.

Unrestricted Fund

Unrestricted funds are the funds for which donors have not imposed any kind of restrictions on their uses (i.e., general fund). The organization is allowed to spend this type of funds based on its greatest need, without any restriction.

Restricted Fund

Restricted funds are to be used only on certain activities and programs in the organization. Restricted funds are the ones whose utilization has been limited by the donor.

These funds are restricted up to a certain period of time. Once the time limit is over, they will become unrestricted funds. The donor may also restrict the use of the funds to support specific activities (i.e., backpacks for back-to-school drive).

These funds may also be used in a designated way and whose principal amount cannot be spent. The income (i.e. interest income) that is generated on the principal amount is then to be used to fund expenses based on the donor's stipulations.

At times donors may restrict funds specifically for fixed assets; for instance, land, building, renovation, etc.

If a donor does not specify any restriction on contribution, it will be treated as an unrestricted asset and will be recorded as unrestricted revenue. The funds will be reported as net assets without restrictions. For restricted contributions, they will be reported as net assets with restrictions.

Fund accounting distinguishes the use of restricted and unrestricted funds. With this method, the organization is able to determine available resources for its ongoing operations and also restricted resources. It also provides audit trail of how money collected from all the funds have been spent for the intended purpose and hence restricted funds can be released.

To summarize, fund accounting allows the users of the financial statements to see clearly what funds have been used and for what purpose. As management of a nonprofit organization, you are responsible for ensuring that all funds received are utilized for the right purpose.

It is interesting to note that, unlike in for-profit businesses, any excess funds that have not been utilized by the nonprofits cannot be distributed to its owners. This is called the inurement constraint. "Inurement" is a term for "benefit." The inurement prohibition forbids the use of the income or assets of a tax-exempt organization to directly or indirectly unduly benefit an individual or other person that has a close relationship with the organization or is able to exercise significant control over the organization. This is an important aspect of fund accounting that helps distinguish nonprofits from profit-oriented organizations.

For example, a nonprofit organization offers daycare services to low-income single mothers in the community for a reduced rate. The organization receive funding to assist the mothers in day care cost for their children. The single mothers who sit on the board would not be able to enroll their children in the organization's day care service at the reduced rate because this would be considered a private inurement. The board members exercise significant control over the organization and/or has a close relationship with the organization and cannot directly or indirectly unduly benefit.

Overview of Financial Statements

Now that we have the basic concept of fund accounting, let us go into the details of the financial statements. The financial statements of nonprofits are similar to the financial statements of a for-profit organization.

They consist of the Statement of Financial Position (similar to the Balance Sheet), the Statement of Activities (similar to the Income Statement) and the cash flow statement. It will, however, not have a statement of changes in equity since a nonprofit does not have shareholders or owners.

Statement of Financial Position

Similar to the balance sheet, the Statement of Financial Position shows users the assets and liabilities owned by the nonprofit. Essentially, it conveys to the users the financial status of the organization.

In the balance sheet of a normal business, you would find three main elements: assets, liabilities, and equity. Yet in the Statement of Financial Position of a nonprofit, you will only see two elements: assets and liabilities, and they can be represented by the following equation:

Assets - Liabilities = Net Assets

A positive net asset position would mean that the organization has more assets than liabilities. This is a desirable position to have for every organization as it means that the board is doing a great job of maintaining the health of the organization's financials.

A negative position would, however, be a reminder to the board of directors that it needs to rebalance its focus and determine how it can improve its financial health.

Note, the Financial Accounting Standards Board requires that the balance sheet of the nonprofits have two classes of net assets:

- Net assets with donor restrictions
- Net assets without donor restrictions

Common line items in this report are:

- Assets
- Cash
- Accounts receivable
- Inventory
- Fixed assets
- Other assets
- Liabilities

Accounts payable

- Accrued expenses
- Sales tax liability
- Income taxes payable
- Debt

Net Assets

- Unrestricted Assets
- Restricted Assets

Statement of Activities

The Statement of Activities, which is similar to the income statement, details the type of income received by the organization and the expenditure section, which lists out the expenses incurred by the nonprofit during the entire accounting period.

The different revenue sources and expenses will be categorized and presented based on their natures. To illustrate, the funds received as a grant will be presented separately from the income raised during a fundraising event. Similarly, for expenses, travelling expenses will be shown in a different line than an expense incurred for printing and stationery.

On the Statement of Activities, nonprofit revenues may be separately presented as the following line items:

- Contributions
- Member dues
- Program fees
- Fundraising events
- Grants
- Investment income
- Gain on sale of investments

Programs are the services that a nonprofit organization provides. In most cases, each program has its own revenue, expenses, and records.

Fundraising refers to actions such as direct mail campaigns and charity events that are meant to raise the organization's profile or solicit donations.

Line items for expenses are also separately presented in detail. At a minimum, the statement of activities usually includes the following line items:

- **Program expenses**. These expenses are incurred in order to deliver specific programs in accordance with the mission of the nonprofit. The presentation may include additional line items to break out the expenses associated with each individual program.
- **Support services expenses.** Those expenses used to manage the organization and raise funds.

The net effect of all revenues and expenses is a change in net assets, not a profit or loss.

At the end of an accounting period, if there is excess income that is unused after deducting all the expenses, the income will be accumulated and recorded as a reserve in the Statement of Financial Position of the organization. This reserve must not be distributed and should be utilized based on its intended purpose in the next accounting period

Statement of Functional Expenses

The statement of functional expenses is also provided and categorizes each of the expenses of the organization to its intended activities. And helps to keep track of fundraising revenue use. Examples of intended activities include programs, fundraising, general, and administrative.

Administration or overhead funds are funds used to manage the operations of a nonprofit organization. These are funds that are required to keep the organization running and must be accounted for and disclosed to contributors. Donors desire that nonprofits maintain their costs, such as salaries, to a minimum so that the majority of donations may go into activities.

One of the biggest mistakes charitable organizations make is misallocating functional expenses. Financial management for nonprofits should ensure that the organization can function and develop. Donors may be hesitant to give if your operational costs become too high.

With donors looking to get the most out of their donations, it's important for organizations to properly manage costs.

Cash flow statement

A cash flow statement shows the movement of cash and cash equivalents coming in and being paid out by the organization. It explains the arrival and use of funds within the organizational activities. It shows ability of the organization to manage its cash flow. This statement is no longer required to be produced by nonprofits but it shows how the organization generates cash and pays debt and liabilities as well as the smooth functioning of its operating activities. The cash movement will commonly be broken down into operating, financing, and investing activities. Here are the descriptions and examples of those activities:

- Operating activities – Any cash inflows or outflows that are related to the operation of the organization. For instance, cash received from donors, cash paid to employees, cash paid to project managers, etc.

- Financing activities – These include all activities that are related to the liabilities of the organization and changes to loans and borrowings. Some examples include interests paid on loans, repayment of advances, drawdown of loans, and so on.

- Investing activities – Investing activities cover cash movement pertaining to investments, such as dividend income, purchase of fixed assets, or proceeds from the sale of investments.

DIFFERENCES BETWEEN ACCOUNTING FOR NONPROFITS AND FOR-PROFITS

Both nonprofit and for-profit organizations are required to submit regular financial reports, and they follow many of the same accounting rules. The two kinds of organizations' goals, however, result in considerable differences in these reports.

A for-profit company's balance sheet details its net equity for owners and shareholders, which equals the organizations assets minus liabilities. Whereas a nonprofit's statement of financial position does not. A nonprofit, on the other hand, does not have shareholders or owners. Instead, it generates a statement of financial position, which lists the company's assets and liabilities.

In for-profit accounting, stockholders' equity is equal to a company's assets minus liabilities. For nonprofits, this section is referred to as net assets. Because there is no equity in a nonprofit, this line item is always referred to as net assets. Temporarily restricted, permanently restricted, and unrestricted net assets are the three types of net assets in this section.

Nonprofit organization's statement of financial position is represented by following equation

$$\textbf{Assets} = \textbf{Liabilities} + \textbf{Net Assets}$$

Because of double-entry bookkeeping, the accounting equation must remain balanced. The items that cause changes in net assets of nonprofit organizations are reported on statement of activities/income and expenditure.

Statement of activities versus income statement: When a corporation tries to make a profit, it creates an income statement that shows its revenues, expenditure, losses, and profits. Because it is driven by a goal rather than the need to generate a profit, a nonprofit does not have a bottom line.

It generates a statement of activities instead of an income statement, which details the revenues and expenditure related with each program. Statement of income and expenditure calculates surplus or deficit in funds/income generated to cover the expenses of an organization's activities. Stakeholders are not seeking profits or surplus, rather they want nonprofit organizations to spend more in social welfare activities. If donors think that a nonprofit organization is carrying a surplus from prior years, it could be implied that the organization is spending less and saving more, and potentially conclude that it doesn't need as much in donations in the future.

Both nonprofits and for-profits are required to track and report their financial flow.

Nonprofits that understand how to handle their data, as well as the insights and results gained from it, will outperform the competition in terms of donor and constituent involvement and organizational viability.

Nonprofits, like any other organization that manages cash flow and pays taxes, should hire a professional accountant.

BENEFITS OF USING ACCOUNTING SOFTWARE

Nonprofit organizations earn income and incur expenses during their operations and their board of directors are required to stay accountable to the stakeholders by applying fund accounting. Hence, it is imperative that nonprofits keep track of their accounting records.

But what is the best way to do that?

In this section, we will discuss why nonprofits should use accounting software to keep track of the accounting records and generating reports.

1) Simplifies work

With accounting software, a lot of work can be automated. The accounting software can help sum totals so that the totals are not calculated by hand, different statements are compiled, and invoices or receipts can be generated.

Not just because it is automated, but because there is a lower risk of mistake due to calculations. That means it will be less likely for a misstatement of actual funds and expenses.

2) More efficient

Reducing the time spent on administrative works will allow organizations to focus on achieving the nonprofits' missions. By using accounting software, all the nonprofits' accounting records can be tracked quicker. The software provides the option to search for transactions in the system without having to dig through different spreadsheets.

Most accounting systems have very friendly user interfaces that let their users key in the business transactions in just a few steps. Opting for cloud-based software, means the organization's bookkeeping can be tracked and reported from just anywhere in the world as long as there is internet connection.

3) Retrieves past records easily

All data that is entered into the accounting system will be available when needed. Accounting software allows its users to look up financial history that its users had previously keyed in with just a few clicks.

You can use those past records to set up a budget for your organization and produce a benchmark for your organization to work on. It will allow more realistic and achievable aims to be formed and help your organization to achieve them.

Furthermore, by keeping accounting records up to date in the accounting software, board members can track the organization's spending within its budget easily. Any deviation can be spotted immediately, allowing your organization to react more quickly to prevent itself from falling into an undesirable financial position.

4) Reduces audit issues

Auditors will always ask for complete accounting records in order for them to carry out an audit. Having accounting software can save you from having to worry about that. When it is time for an audit, you simply have to open up your software, print out the relevant records and hand it to your auditor.

Preparing accounting records by hand may often result in more misstatements than using accounting software. Detection of misstatements will usually cause an auditor to perform an even more detailed audit than usual as they may be concerned of missing material misstatements. Using accounting software can help lower the chance of that happening.

Nonprofit founders and executives tend to wear many hats. Often, their primary hat isn't that of a financial guru. That's why nonprofit tax software is indispensable for tax-exempt organizations.

NONPROFITS' NEED FOR
ACCOUNTANTS

Many nonprofit organizations do not include a professional accountant in their annual budget to manage their financial operations. Often, these tasks are delegated to an unskilled employee or volunteer. This mistake is one of the most common made by nonprofit organizations.

If bookkeeping and accounting are not correctly managed, nonprofits are at risk of fraudulent activities. This can happen frequently, especially if the finances aren't monitored regularly or personnel lacks experience. A large portion of a nonprofit's staff consists of volunteers. Volunteers may leave unexpectedly and cause gaps in documentation.

Nonprofit accounting is different than for-profit accounting and requires a special skill set. Hiring a professional means that someone with the necessary expertise and experience is constantly monitoring the accounts and may discover anything that an inexperienced person would overlook. Many organizations, for example, meet the standards for unintentionally using temporarily restricted cash, but are unaware of it since no one is keeping track.

Too often, temporarily restricted funds are forgotten until cash flow requirements become pressing. Keeping an up-to-date company schedule assists managers to better estimate their operating demands by knowing what funds are available.

A nonprofit accountant is detailed and analytical. They can be considered a numbers detective. While a nonprofit bookkeeper records nonprofit data. An accountant has the educational background necessary to take the analysis of that data to another level. An accountant is responsible for duties such as:

Reviewing all accounts. Accountants will ensure the financial transactions are recorded correctly in the nonprofit's accounting records to make sure the organization is on track for future goals.

Balancing both sides of a financial transaction. Accountants handle the balancing of both the credit and debit sides of a double-entry bookkeeping system.

Determining how transactions affects your accounting records. Nonprofit accountants help determine the financial health organizations and how each transaction affects the well-being.

Understanding the "why" of accounting situations. Not only does the accountant need to understand, but they also need to explain it to other staff and board members clearly.

Preparing detailed reports. Accountants compile comprehensive reports explaining an organization's transactions, usually on a monthly or quarterly basis.

Comparing actual vs. budgeted expenses/income. Nonprofit accountants help nonprofits understand where the actual expenses/income differ from the budgeted.

Comparing actual expenses and income year-to-year. Comparing your nonprofit's current expenses and income to those from previous years can help create more accurate predictions for the future.

Preparing your books for audit. A nonprofit accountant will make sure everything in the transaction history matches the financial books so that it's ready for an annual audit.

Filing your nonprofit's Form 990. All nonprofits must file an annual Form 990 in order to report financial data back to the government and maintain their 501(C)(3) status. An accountant will help a nonprofit ensure this tax form is in order each year.

Reconcile all bank accounts. Accountants match the cash balances on the balance sheet to the bank account records, resolving any discrepancies between the two reports.

Review all bank accounts to ensure they meet GAAP compliance standards. Nonprofit accountants will keep a nonprofit up to accepted industry reporting standards.

As you can see, accountants take the data recorded by nonprofit bookkeepers in order to analyze it and create actionable steps for the organization. The nonprofit accountant can also perform the role of the nonprofit bookkeeper. In addition, an accountant will interpret, classify, and summarize your financial data correctly.

Accountants prepare record transactions with the thought of compliance and the long-term sustainability of the organization in mind. Their concern is that the 501c3 status is maintained by submitting a correct Form 990 on time and that the organization passes a routine audit without difficulty.

At the very least, make sure you have a CPA who will walk the board of directors through all of the numbers, ensuring that you understand the Statement of Activities, the Statement of Financial Position, and Cash Flow Statement. The more knowledgeable the board becomes, the more empowered it is to make financial decisions that will lead to the organization's success.

DIFFERENCE BETWEEN AN AUDIT, REVIEW, AND COMPILATION

If your nonprofit organization wants to improve the credibility of the financial statements, your organization can engage a CPA to prepare its financial statements.

A CPA can provide three different levels of views of financial statements. These three views are Audits, Reviews, and Compilations. An audit is the most thorough, followed by a more involved review, and lastly is a basic compilation report.

Audit

An independent audit is not the same as an IRS audit. Rather, it is an examination of your accounting records and financial statements by an independent auditor—normally, a CPA. The auditor is an independent professional hired and paid by the nonprofit. The auditor will do an independent investigation to test the accuracy of the accounting records and internal controls.

The level of assurance provided by a CPA by performing an audit is the highest. It requires the CPA to obtain a lot more evidence than the other types of services to corroborate the financial statements produced by an organization. An audit is usually demanded by users who have concerns over the financial position of an organization.

Some of the work that an auditor might perform includes:

- Obtaining third-party confirmations such as bank confirmations, payable or receivable confirmations, and so on.

- Testing internal controls and systems of an organization to determine if they are effective in supporting the organization's daily operations

- Substantive analytical procedures to understand how any changes in your organization's operation can affect the figures reported in the financial statements

- Examining supporting documents, such as donation receipts, invoices, etc., for selected transactions

- Viewing of physical assets to ensure their existence

At the conclusion of the audit, the auditor issues a report in the form of a letter stating whether, in the auditor's professional judgment, the accounting records and year-end financial statements fairly represent the nonprofit's financial position according to GAAP and free of material misstatement. The auditor's letter is attached to the front of your financial statements. A clean bill of health from an auditor shows the world that you're keeping your books in a responsible manner.

Due to the high level of assurance required, an audit will take the most substantial amount of time to complete compared to the others. As such, it will also cost more to your organization.

Review

A review will result in the CPA offering limited assurance on your organization's financial statements. The CPA will perform only analytical procedures and determine if the financial statements are reasonably stated.

Analytical procedures involve inquiring the organization's management as to whether the numbers presented in the financial statements are correct and determining whether such information provided by the management makes sense.

Since only analytical procedures will be performed, the CPA will incur much fewer hours than with an audit and will therefore charge a lower price to perform a review than an audit for your organization.

There are two primary distinctions between the two: First, a review is often half the price of an audit. Second, a review is exactly that – a review. In contrast to an audit, with a review, the CPA does not do extensive "testing." They look for substantial flaws and obvious GAAP violations. They won't, however, go in and test individual transactions in the same way that an audit would. A review gives some assurance, but it does not validate transactions independently.

Compilation

If your organization does not require any assurance on the financial statements and simply want a CPA to help compile the financial statements into a format that complies with GAAP, then you should ask for a compilation.

The CPA will then take the financial data recorded and provided by your organization at their face values and put them together into the desired format. No testing or any procedure will be performed. A letter will then be attached to the financial statements to show that it has been prepared by a CPA.

This is the simplest of all three views and will require the fewest hours to perform. The cost will also be the cheapest among the three options.

Is an Audit Necessary?

Nonprofit organizations typically ask if they require an audit or a review. State restrictions, the necessity for a Federal A-133, or the criteria of certain funders can all influence this question.

When making this decision, each organization should be mindful of the state laws as well as the expectations of funders – both existing and future prospects.

Ensure that your organization is following government regulations that are specific to your organization and location. Also, be proactive in learning the requirements of your funders. (For example, the United Way demands a review for smaller organizations and an audit for larger organizations.) Make sure you read the tiny print on the grant application so you know what you're getting into.

Many nonprofits may determine that the cost of an audit surpasses the grant's benefits. If the grant is $10,000 and the audit will cost you $8,000, it is unlikely that the effort will be worthwhile.

Keeping track of all of these rules might be difficult, so ensuring the organization has a well-informed Finance Committee or a financial professional who can assist will be very beneficial.

As a nonprofit organization that relies on public donations and funds to run its operation, it is vital to practice accountability.

Ways audit services benefit your nonprofit

In many of the most fundamental ways, a nonprofit is run in an entirely different way than a for-profit organization, ranging from its organizational structure to management. However, some of the same rules still apply. In some states, the law may require audits, while in others, it is not necessary to conduct one. Although, it is not a bad idea to consider having an audit completed anyway if you plan to apply for government funding or if you wish to maintain a good reputation with the public. Below are a few other reasons your nonprofit might consider obtaining audit of its financial statements.

Abiding by State Law. Laws vary by state not only in regard to whether or not nonprofit organizations are required to be audited, but also under which circumstances. In most states, nonprofits are required to submit reports to have the ability to fundraise. Other reasons certain states require them include meeting or exceeding a threshold for charitable donations, the total amount of fiscal year revenue, charity registration renewal, and other indicators. The type of assurance service required varies, also. In some states, depending on the circumstances, a full audit is required. Other states or different circumstances require only a review or a compilation.

Maintaining a Good Reputation. When nonprofit organizations are in the news, it's often not because of charitable deeds or honorable accomplishments. It's because they are being accused of or being investigated for fraud. Seeking audit services is a good way to help prevent a situation like this from occurring. The public, especially those who contribute or have contributed to charitable organizations, appreciate financial transparency. People want access to information, and when they're denied access, they may feel that you have something to hide. Keeping financial records available to the public can help avoid this issue.

Applying for Funding. If a charitable organization is hoping to apply for a grant or other funding, there's a good chance an audit may be needed. Many agencies, especially the state or federal government, want proof that a nonprofit runs a tight ship before providing funding of any kind. Some private organizations do, too. If you're up for a substantial grant or plan to apply for funding now or in the future, it's a smart idea to begin conducting them annually. Showing that you conduct your financial business by the book is always advantageous.

Demonstrating transparency. One of the methods to practice accountability is by performing an audit, even though it is not required by law. An audit will allow organizations to show that it is transparent about its finances.

This will make it easier for organizations to obtain funding and donations. It also shows accountability and improves the public's trust in charitable organization.

When requested, organizations should allow the public to have a copy of financial statements and audit reports.

Because nonprofits have a completely different financial culture than for-profit businesses, it seems strange that it would be necessary for a nonprofit to conduct an annual audit. However, despite the fact that it is mandatory by law under certain circumstances in some states, it's often simply a matter of good business practice to choose some kind of regular audit services, be it a full audit, a review, or a compilation. Proving your organization to be fiscally responsible and reliable is an easy way to open the door to funding opportunities and to maintain a positive image with the public and, especially, with your contributors.

THE IMPORTANCE OF ADHERING TO REGULATORY REQUIREMENTS

Nonprofit organizations that do not adhere to regulatory reporting requirements face financial penalties that will not only destroy capital but also limit their ability to serve important stakeholders.

Further, any hint of mismanagement of funds, whether through negligence or otherwise, can be extremely detrimental to an organization's credibility with relevant stakeholders. Because of this, providing transparency and eagerly anticipating regulatory needs in terms of financial reporting will not only save a nonprofit money, but also help ensure its ability to operate in the future.

Conflict of interest. The board of directors is hired for their experience, resources that they can provide to the organization, and their connections. This may, however, sometimes create a conflict of interest between the directors and the organizations they are with.

For example, your nonprofit purchases certain goods or services from a company related to one of the directors while such goods or services could actually be obtained elsewhere with a much lower cost or better quality.

The board of directors should ensure that it practices accountability in this kind of situation and make decisions based on the best interest of the organization, not on its own interests. This is the fiduciary responsibility of a director of a nonprofit organization.

Directors should refrain from any activities that may result in a conflict of interest between their own and that of the organization.

Donors' personal information. When collecting donations from donors, nonprofit organizations may come across various personal information of the donors. Some of them include sensitive information such as bank details, credit card information, email addresses, and the home addresses of the donors.

To protect the donors' private information is not only important, but an ethical act. Everyone in the organization should be responsible for ensuring that such information stays in the organization and shall not be misused for any personal gain.

Especially in this digital age, if your organization is utilizing an online platform to accept donations, you should make sure your website's security is regularly reviewed to prevent any data leakage that might jeopardize the trust of your donors.

Good management. Regular reviews of the organization's board performance are also useful in ensuring the board is doing a decent job in making sure that the organization heading in the right direction.

Such practice can help to prevent the board from being sidetracked and allow the organization to make the highest impact possible in its own area of specialization.

Management's pay. Excessive benefits for those who manage a nonprofit organization may lead to dissatisfaction among the donors. Such benefits may include luxury traveling fees, paid vacations, and so on.

This might affect the trust of the public and is not healthy for the success and the growth of the organization. Hence, the board should be very transparent in terms of management's compensation and steer clear of any misappropriation of money.

FORM 990 DEFINED

The tax system for nonprofit's can be complicated, and tax law revisions can have an impact on anything from how you report your income to how you manage volunteers. Some of a nonprofit's income, for example, may be taxable. The regulations governing how nonprofits must handle and report income can change whenever new tax regulations are passed.

Nonprofits must also keep careful record and report the value of some employee benefits, which, if not correctly recorded, might be considered taxable income.

Nonprofit taxes consist of more than just reporting spending and gifts. The tracking of labor and services is also required. The unpaid labor, provided by volunteers, has value that might affect the organization's taxes and expenses.

The market value of in-kind services provided can diminish the percentage of administrative and managerial costs that is directly paid for by the organization's monetary contributions.

Nonprofits must build a system to manage and record their work in order to ensure correct tax reporting and to ensure that volunteers provide the most value. Regular bookkeeping and accounting activities should include updating these records, and the tracking system should be standardized across the organization.

Net assets should be categorized according to whether they are restricted (either by donors or grant terms) or unrestricted in a nonprofit's statement of financial situation.

Nonprofit board members may find government compliance documents to be complex and confusing. The fact that the laws and rules are constantly changing may make them even more difficult. This makes it difficult for boards to finish tasks correctly, especially when the board directorship has changed many times. However, it is the board's responsibility to guarantee that compliance documentation is completed and submitted on time. One of the most significant documents that nonprofit board members are responsible for is the IRS Form 990.

Despite the complicated terms and questions that Form 990 contains, it serves a very important purpose for the government and the general public.

What is the purpose of Form 990? The IRS and the general public can use the information in the document to assess the strength and profitability of organizations. Your Form 990 can be an effective public relations tool for demonstrating that your nonprofit is well run.

FORM 990 AND HOW IT WORKS

Form 990, officially known as the "Return of Organization Exempt from Income Tax," is the information return filed yearly by tax-exempt nonprofits with the IRS. In simple terms, it's a federal informational return that discloses financial and other data about your nonprofit to the general public. It contains information of your organization on whether it is:

- Serving the mission for which the IRS granted it tax-exempt status.
- Complying with federal tax law on various aspects.
- Implementing best governance practices and adhering to written policies that demonstrate accountability and transparency.

The Form 990 collects comprehensive information about the mission, programs, and finances of the nonprofit and provides an opportunity to report what it accomplished the prior year, thus making a case for keeping its tax-exempt status. In addition, most states use the Form 990 for regulatory oversight of state income tax filing requirements for organizations claiming exemption from state income tax.

In a variety of ways, your organization can use Form 990 to communicate with its members and the general public. For instance, your organization could:

- Provide financial information showing appropriate financial care of members' donations and contributions. Members want to know that the money they pay is being properly utilized for the organization's missions.

- Inform members of the organization's mission, offer a thorough narrative of the organization's activities and achievements throughout the reporting period, and demonstrate how the organization provides value to its members.

- Show the commitment to responsible governance by following all applicable laws and regulations and applying the best practices for a nonprofit organization. In Form 990, you can explain how any conflict of interests is handled, how executive pay and benefits are set, and also how Form 990 is reviewed before filing with IRS. All of these show the commitment, as the directors or founders, to ascertaining if fiduciary duties have been performed by the members and the organization.

As the leaders of a nonprofit organization, the yearly filing of Form 990 should be used to remind members and board of directors of what the organization is and could be. Form 990 could serve as a springboard for an organization to become more responsible, transparent, and a well-governed organization.

Tip: When completing Form 990, be sure to provide all requested information. The IRS isn't shy about returning incomplete forms or requesting additional information if everything needed is not provided on the first attempt. The IRS will return the Form 990 filing and require the information to be resubmitted to avoid any penalties.

Do charitable organizations have to pay taxes? Even though nonprofit organizations generally do not pay federal taxes, the Form 990 is an important compliance requirement for nonprofit boards. Even organizations that are exempt from paying federal income tax have to report their activities annually to the IRS. Often the Form 990 is the only source of this information and, as such, it safeguards nonprofits to ensure that they conduct their business in a way that is consistent with their public responsibilities. The form also serves as a deterrent to nonprofits abusing their tax-exempt status. The federal government is still interested in how nonprofits manage their funds, but not in general.

In essence, the federal government recognizes the importance of nonprofit organizations in their communities. As a result, the IRS requires the Form 990 to ensure that your nonprofit is functioning in a legal and appropriate manner. The board of directors are responsible for ensuring that Form 990 is correctly completed and filed on time each year.

Form 990 must be made public. It helps donors and other interested people find and support reliable charity organizations. It's critical to make your Form 990 public because the information on it holds your organization accountable for the work it does to founders and stakeholders. It explains what programs and activities are offered, how money is made, and potentially how long the organization can last. The general public utilizes this data to assist them in deciding which charity to fund. It provides an easy, convenient way for donors and other people interested in supporting a particular cause to identify and evaluate the best nonprofits to support. Since an organization can clarify its mission on the Form 990 and detail its accomplishments of the previous year, donors can learn where the group generates and spends its revenue.

A donor foundation can see just how sustainable the nonprofit might be by having access to its cash reserves, which demonstrate for potential donors and employees how well the nonprofit pays its top employees and how financially stable it is.

Candidates for board member positions will almost certainly look over the Form 990. It provides insights that can used by potential board members to determine who else is on the board and how robust the cash reserves are.

Since the Form 990 provides such critical information about the organization, it is easy to see that it can be a brilliant public relations tool for the organization when care is taken to fill it out accurately, carefully, and on time. Nonprofit organizations simplify their intended purpose and achievement details from last year on Form 990.

WHAT NONPROFIT BOARD MEMBERS SHOULD KNOW ABOUT FORM 990

Board of Directors should seek to learn the answers to the following questions because the nonprofit's Form 990 is such an important compliance responsibility:

What is the purpose of Form 990?

Who is required to file Form 990?

Who is not required to file Form 990?

When is the deadline for filing Form 990?

To what address should Form 990 be sent?

All of these are excellent questions. In most circumstances, an outside CPA will complete the form, although it can also be completed by the board or a board committee. In either instance, it is the board's responsibility to thoroughly analyze Form 990 and ensure that it is delivered by the deadline.

Following that, boards must make their IRS Form 990 available to the public. Here are some ideas for how to go about it:

- Create a link to it on your website.

- Make it a part of one of your facilities' offerings.

- Consult your listing on GuideStar, a website that compiles data on nonprofits.

Keep in mind that during regular business hours, you must make your Form 990 and tax-exemption application available to the public. It's against the law to charge for it. The IRS website also allows interested groups and individuals to access your Form 990.

Charities that are required to file a Form 990

Nonprofit is an inclusive phrase that encompasses many different types of organizations. A Form 990 is not required for all nonprofits. However, most charitable nonprofits that are recognized as tax-exempt are required to file an annual informational return with the IRS.

Here's a basic rundown of who must file Form 990:

- Private foundations (Form 990-PF, regardless of income)
- Almost all tax-exempt organizations with gross receipts of at least $200,000 and assets of at least $500,000 are required (Form 990)
- Nonprofits having gross receipts of $50,000 or more are considered large (Form 990 or Form 990-EZ)
- Nonprofits having gross receipts of $50,000 or less are considered smaller (990-N which is an e-Postcard)
- Organizations that do not qualify for an exemption under Section 501(c), 527, or 4947(a)(1) of the U.S. tax law.

There are a few exceptions to the rule when it comes to Form 990 filing. Nonprofits that fall within the following categories are excluded from filing the form:

- Most faith-based organizations, including churches (religious schools, missions, missionary organizations)
- Other nonprofits' subsidiaries (the parent group files Form 990 on their behalf).
- Universities (i.e., state-run institutions).
- Governmental organizations.
- Political committees.

If any board member is unsure whether or not your organization is required to submit Form 990, check the list of exceptions and record it in your board meeting minutes. Your nonprofit's tax-exempt status could be jeopardized if you fail to file the required IRS forms.

Form 990 (full form)

The IRS requires an extensive amount of information from the organization; the instructions for how to complete the 12-page form are 100 pages in length. Additionally, the organization can be subject to a large penalty if it does not file on time.

Form 990 consists of 12 different parts:

Part I is a summary of the organization. It requires information about the organization's activities and governance (e.g., mission statement, number of employees and volunteers, etc.), revenue, expenses, and net assets or fund balances.

Part II is the signature block where an officer of the organization attests under penalty of perjury that the information is true, correct, and complete to the best of their knowledge.

Part III is a statement of the organization's accomplishments, including the mission statement and the expenses and revenues for the organization's three largest program services.

Part IV is a checklist of schedules that must be completed and accompany the form (explained later).

Part V is for statements about other IRS filings and tax compliance. For example, if the organization can receive tax-deductible contributions, it must indicate if donors were provided with the required confirmation for their donations.

Part VI asks for information about the governing body, policies, and procedures, as well as the management of the organization.

Part VII lists the compensation paid to current and former officers, directors, trustees, key employees, employees receiving more than $100,000 in compensation, and up to five independent contractors receiving more than $100,000 in payment from the organization.

Part VIII is a statement of the organization's revenue from related or exempt funds and unrelated business income, which requires the filing of Form 990-T; this income is not exempt.

Part IX is for reporting the organization's expenses.

Part X is the organization's balance sheet.

Part XI is a reconciliation of the net assets of the organization.

Part XII explains the organization's financial statements and reporting (e.g., whether it uses the cash, accrual, or another method of reporting to prepare the form and whether its financial statements were compiled and reviewed by an independent accountant).

In addition to Form 990, the organization may be required to attach various schedules – A through O and R – to the form in order to provide supplemental information. The organization can determine the schedules they are required to use based on answers to questions throughout the form.

Form 990-EZ

Instead of completing the full Form 990, an organization may be eligible to complete a simplified version of Form 990, called Form 990-EZ: Short Form Return of Organization Exempt from Income Tax. This is a four-page informational form, rather than a 12-page form, and requires some of the same information as Form 990. The 990-EZ can be used by an organization with gross receipts of less than $200,000 and total assets of less than $500,000 at the end of the tax year. Comparable to Form 990, Form 990-EZ is also available to the public.

The 990EZ is like the little brother of the standard Form 990, but that doesn't mean it's less important!

Throughout this four-page form, there are other questions that the IRS asks to gain additional insights into your organization's mission and financial situation. In addition to the primary questions, they'll ask you for detailed information regarding:

Completing the Heading of Form 990-EZ

1. The nonprofit's EIN and the organization's Taxpayer Identification Number (TIN).
2. The tax year being filed.
3. The legal name, mailing address for the organization, and telephone number.
4. Any other names the organization may use.
5. The name and address of the principal officer.
6. The website for the organization.
7. Confirmation that the organization's annual gross receipts are under $200,000.
8. Accounting method (i.e., cash, accrual or other)
9. Organization structure (i.e., corporation, association, trust, etc.)

In addition to the basic information that you'd need for the Form 990-N (listed above), you'll also need the following to file your Form 990-EZ:

Part I list the revenue, expenses, and changes in net assets or fund balances (Statement of Activities) of the organization.

Part II is the organization's balance sheets (Statement of Financial Position).

Part III is a Statement of Program Service Accomplishments and includes a statement of the organization's accomplishments, including the mission statement, donated products and services, and the expenses and revenues for the organization's three largest program services.

Part IV is a list of officers, directors, trustees, and key employees, even if they are not compensated.

Part V Other Information asks for information about the governing body, policies, and procedures, as well as the management of the organization.

Part VI Section 501(c)(3) Organizations Only – the organization's lobbying activities are disclosed, along with a list of officers, directors, trustees, and key employees that includes the compensation paid to current and former officers, directors, trustees, key employees, employees receiving more than $100,000 in compensation, and up to five independent contractors receiving more than $100,000 in payment from the organization.

In addition to this information, there is also a dedicated list of "schedules" that might also be needed to be completed. If your organization meets certain criteria, the IRS might ask for supplementary information to fill in some of the information gaps. For example, the schedules include:

- Schedule of Contributors (a list of your contributors)
- Schedule D to provide more details regarding your financial statements
- Schedule F to report activities that occur outside of the country
- Schedule G to describe your organization's fundraising activities

Signature Block, where an officer of the organization attests under penalty of perjury that the information is true, correct, and complete to the best of their knowledge.

Form 990-N

Small tax-exempt organizations are usually eligible to file Form 990-N to satisfy their annual reporting requirement, if their annual gross receipts are normally $50,000 or less.

Gross receipts are the total amounts the organization received from all sources during its annual tax or calendar year, without subtracting any costs or expenses.

Gross receipts are considered to be normally $50,000 or less if the organization:

- Has been in existence for one year or less and received, or donors have pledged to give, $75,000 or less during its first taxable year;

- Has been in existence between one and three years and averaged $60,000 or less in gross receipts during each of its first two tax years; and

- Is at least three years old and averaged $50,000 or less in gross receipts for the immediately preceding three tax years (including the year for which calculations are being made).

Form 990-N is easy to complete. You'll need only eight items of basic information about your organization.

1. The nonprofit's EIN and the organization's TIN.
2. The tax year being filed.
3. The legal name and mailing address for the organization.
4. Any other names the organization may use.
5. The name and address of the principal officer.
6. The website for the organization.
7. Confirmation that the organization's annual gross receipts are under $50,000.
8. If applicable, a statement if the organization is going out of business.

Please note, an organization eligible to submit Form 990-N can instead choose to file Form 990 or Form 990-EZ to satisfy its annual reporting requirement. If you choose to file an annual information return (Form 990 or Form 990-EZ) instead of the e-Postcard, you must file a complete return. An incomplete or partially completed Form 990 or Form 990-EZ will not satisfy the annual filing requirement. Also, you may be assessed a late filing penalty if you file Form 990 or Form 990-EZ late.

Although the Form 990-N is a less complicated way to report the nonprofit activities and to stay in compliance with the IRS, especially if your organization didn't raise a lot of funds in the past year, the disadvantages of filing Form 990-N is that it doesn't bring any information to potential donors on the activities, financial information, and accomplishments of the organization.

Organizations that provide grants often request a Form 990-EZ from the 501(c)(3) that is seeking the grant. The Form 990-EZ provides a lot of information about the activities and finances of the organization.

Form 990-N, Electronic Notice (e-Postcard), is submitted electronically; there are no paper forms.

Some organizations aren't eligible to use Form 990-N even if their gross receipts are normally $50,000 or less. These organizations must file different forms instead to satisfy their annual reporting requirement. The following organizations cannot file Form 990-N (the e-Postcard), but must file different forms instead:

- Gross receipts are over $50,000: Tax-exempt organizations with annual gross receipts that are normally greater than $50,000 must file Form 990 PDF or Form 990-EZ PDF.

- Private foundations must file Form 990-PF PDF.

- Supporting organizations: Most section 509(a)(3) supporting organizations are required to file Form 990 or Form 990-EZ.

- Small organizations (those whose annual gross receipts are normally not more than $5,000) that support certain religious organizations must file Form 990-N unless they voluntarily file Form 990 or Form 990-EZ.

- Section 527 (political) organizations required to file an annual exempt organization return must file Form 990 or Form 990-EZ.

Other ineligible organizations: Other organization types that are ineligible to submit a Form 990-N include:

- Section 501(c)(1) – U.S. government instrumentalities
- Section 501(c)(20) – Group legal services plans
- Section 501(c)(23) – Pre-1880 Armed Forces organizations
- Section 501(c)(24) – ERISA sec. 4049 trusts
- Section 501(d) – Religious and apostolic organizations
- Section 529 – Qualified tuition programs
- Section 4947(a)(2) – Split-interest trusts
- Section 4947(a)(1) – Charitable trusts treated as private foundations

Part of the stress that comes with tax forms is the old adage: garbage in, garbage out. This means the form, regardless of 990-N, 990-EZ or 990, is only as good as the information you put in it.

By ensuring that throughout the year that revenue, expenses, and changes in net assets are correct, the form becomes a simple plug-and-play for the preparer.

UNRELATED BUSINESS TAXABLE INCOME DEFINED

Even though a nonprofit organization is recognized as tax exempt, taxes may still be owed on its unrelated business income. For most nonprofit organizations, unrelated business income is income that is regularly earned from a trade or business that is not substantially related to the charitable, educational, or other purpose on which the organization's exemption is based.

Tax-exempt nonprofit organizations generally function for charitable or other beneficial community purposes, so most income that they receive is exempt from taxes under the Internal Revenue Code. However, income-producing activities that are perceived to be "unrelated to their exempt purposes" may result in taxable income.

Unrelated business taxable income (UBTI) prevents or limits tax-exempt entities from engaging in businesses that are unrelated to their primary purposes. Most forms of passive income, such as dividends, interest income, and capital gains from the sale or exchange of capital assets, are not treated as UBTI.

Unrelated business income is the income from a trade or business regularly conducted by a tax-exempt organization and not substantially related to the performance by the organization of its exempt purpose or function. Use by the organization of the profits derived from this activity does not, alone, make the activity substantially related to the performance by the organization of its exempt purpose or function.

Income generated from eligible taxable activities are subject to an estimated tax of 21% on income, with the passage of the Tax Cuts and Jobs Act of 2017. The tax law change imposes a tax on nonprofits at the new corporate rate of 21% on income from each unrelated business activity separately. Therefore, it is expected that income and losses from each individual business activity will need to be reported separately, and losses from one may not be used to offset income from the other business activities. This means that it is important for all nonprofits' with unrelated business income to carefully track the expenses involved in producing the specific unrelated business income, so that those expenses can be used to offset gains from that specific activity.

A tax-exempt nonprofit organization that receives $1,000 or more of gross income from an unrelated business must file the additional tax return Form 990-T with the IRS. A nonprofit organization must pay estimated tax if the tax due for the year is expected to be $500 or more.

The responsibility to file Form 990-T is in addition to the obligation to file the annual information return, Form 990, 990-EZ or 990-PF. Each organization must file a separate Form 990-T, except titleholding corporations and organizations receiving their earnings that file a consolidated return under Internal Revenue Code section 1501.

Charitable nonprofits filing the IRS Form 990-T must also make this form available for public inspection when requested.

Every charitable nonprofit should be focused on knowing where its income is being derived. It should be determined whether any of the income is taxable under the unrelated business income tax "UBIT" guidelines to avoid any potential tax liability for unrelated business income.

Trade or business. The term "trade or business" generally includes any activity conducted for the creation of income from selling goods or performing services. An activity must be conducted with intent to make a profit to establish a trade or business. An activity does not lose its identity as a trade or business simply because it is done within a larger group of similar activities that may or may not be related to the tax-exempt purposes of the organization.

For example, the regular sale of coffee to the general public by a church doesn't lose its identity as a trade or business, even though the church also provides coffee to the parishioners of the church on Sunday mornings in accordance with its exempt purpose. Similarly, soliciting, selling, and publishing commercial advertising is a trade or business even though the advertising is published in a tax-exempt organization's annual souvenir book provided at its fundraiser that contains information regarding the organization's exempt purpose.

Regularly conducted. Business activities of tax-exempt organizations ordinarily are considered regularly conducted if they show a frequency and continuity, and are operated similar to comparable commercial activities of nonexempt organizations.

For example, an organization helping the homeless that volunteers to work behind the vending stand at the stadium for two weeks would not be considered conducting a regular a trade or business. Volunteering as a vendor would not compete with similar business that is a non-exempt organization that would ordinarily operate year-round. However, operating a commercial parking lot every Saturday, year-round, would be the regular conduct of a trade or business.

Not substantially related. A business activity isn't substantially related to an organization's tax-exempt purpose if it doesn't contribute significantly to accomplishing that purpose (other than through the production of funds). Whether an activity contributes importantly depends on the facts involved.

In determining whether activities contribute significantly to the accomplishment of an exempt purpose, the size and extent of the activities involved must be considered in relation to the nature and extent of the exempt function that they intend to serve. For example, to the degree an activity is performed on a scale larger than is reasonably necessary to perform an exempt purpose, it doesn't contribute significantly to the accomplishment of the exempt purpose. The part of the activity that is more than needed to accomplish the exempt purpose is an unrelated trade or business.

Also, in determining whether activities contribute significantly to the accomplishment of an exempt purpose, the following principles apply.

Selling of products of tax-exempt functions.

Generally, selling products that result from the performance of a tax-exempt functions isn't an unrelated trade or business if the product is sold in substantially the same state it is in when the exempt functions are completed. Thus, for an exempt organization engaged in teaching art to underprivileged children (its exempt function), selling articles made by these children as part of their program services is not an unrelated trade or business.

However, if a completed product resulting from a tax-exempt activity is used or exploited in further business activity beyond what is reasonably appropriate or necessary to dispose of it as is, the activity is an unrelated trade or business. For example, if a tax-exempt organization teaches inner city youth how to cook, the sale of the meals created in the ordinary course of operation of the project isn't an unrelated trade or business. But if the organization uses the meals along with other meals created by chefs not enrolled in the program to sell the food items in a full-time restaurant, the operation of a full-time restaurant outside of the program operations is an unrelated trade or business, unless the manufacturing activities themselves contribute significantly to the accomplishment of an exempt purpose of the organization.

Dual use of assets or facilities. If an asset or facility necessary to the conduct a tax-exempt activity is also used in commercial activities, its use for exempt functions doesn't, by itself, make the commercial activities a related trade or business. The test, as discussed earlier, is whether the activities contribute importantly to the accomplishment of exempt purposes.

For example, a school K-8 has an auditorium that it uses as gymnasium for the students. The auditorium operates continuously while the school is open to the children. If the organization also operates the auditorium as a rental space on the weekend for churches to meet when the school is closed, the activity is an unrelated trade or business.

Exploitation of tax-exempt functions. Tax-exempt activities sometimes create goodwill or other intangibles that can be exploited in a commercial way. When an organization exploits such an intangible in commercial activities, the fact that the income depends in part upon a tax-exempt function of the organization doesn't make the commercial activities a related trade or business. Unless the commercial exploitation contributes importantly to the accomplishment of the exempt purpose, the commercial activities are an unrelated trade or business.

Reporting of Corporate Sponsorships

Nonprofits receiving corporate sponsorship income should determine whether the income received as sponsorship money is considered a tax-free gift (e.g., a charitable contribution) or as taxable advertising payments which may trigger unrelated business income taxes.

Both charitable nonprofits and the corporate sponsor usually assume the income is a charitable contribution. However, unless the payment is designed to meet IRS requirements of a "qualified sponsorship payment," the payment will probably be classified as taxable income. The Internal Revenue Code Section 513(i) defines a "qualified sponsorship payment" as any payment made by any person engaged in a trade or business with respect to which there is no arrangement or expectation that such person will receive any substantial return benefit other than the use or acknowledgement of the name or logo (or product lines) of such person's trade or business in connection with the activities of the organization that receives such payment.

Such use or acknowledgement does not include advertising of an individual or business's products or services (including messages containing qualitative or comparative language, price information, or other indications of savings or value, an endorsement, or an inducement to purchase, sell, or use such products or services). If the corporate sponsor has any expectation of receiving a "substantial return benefit" for its payment, the payment will result in taxable income for the nonprofit and will require the income to be reported to IRS on Form 990-T.

A great way prevent paying taxes on corporate sponsorship is by ensuring corporate sponsorship payments meet the definition of "qualified sponsorship payments." A qualified sponsorship payment is acknowledged by the charitable nonprofit in the same way as any other charitable donation.

Review how the nonprofit organization acknowledges regular donors compared to how the corporate sponsor is recognized. Is there a difference? Is the difference in acknowledgement for the corporate sponsor similar to any of the factors described below?

Situations that may result in taxable income.

Exclusiveness: the IRS determines exclusivity to be a significant benefit to a for-profit business. So, if a nonprofit promises a for-profit organization to be the "exclusive" sponsor, that promise creates an automatic finding of "substantial return benefit." In addition, the use of the word "endorse" can similarly imply a substantial benefit to the company that is being endorsed.

- Offering incentives to purchase a sponsor's products or services.

- Providing a link from a sponsor's name/logo on the nonprofit's website to the page of a sponsor's website where a product or service is sold, or listing the telephone number where the merchandise or service are often ordered.

- Offering more than nominal services or other privileges to a sponsor compensates for its sponsorship payment.

- Receiving payments from corporate sponsor that's based on the number of attendees at the nonprofit's event.

- Providing sponsors specific advertising opportunities, at no cost, in regularly scheduled publications that normally require a paid fee for advertising.

- Factors that usually indicate contributions as charitable:

- Acknowledgement of corporate sponsor by including the sponsor's name, logo, general phone number, locations, and internet address in printed media, or on a nonprofit's website.

- Value-neutral displays of a sponsor's products or services, or the distribution of free samples of a sponsor's products at a nonprofit's event. The nonprofit should not endorse the product/service.

- A single stationary website link that takes the viewer only to the corporate sponsor's home page – not to a page where a product or service is marketed or sold.

Some payments are both taxable and non-taxable.

Income received from a business sponsor can actually be a mixture of charitable contributions and advertising payments. When this happens, a portion of the sponsorship income will be taxable. For example, acknowledging a corporate sponsor's support for a conference or special event with a banner and a public "thank you" from the stage, if the sponsorship "package" also includes a full page "ad" in the conference souvenir book, with text written by the corporation that advertises its products and services to attendees at the conference. At least some portion of the corporate sponsorship payment should be considered advertising income for the promotion in the souvenir book.

222

In this situation, the nonprofit will have to report the advertising portion of the income as "unrelated business income" (UBI), subject to UBIT.

THE IMPORTANCE OF THE TIMELINESS OF FORM 990

Knowing the deadline for filing Form 990 is critical for nonprofit board members. When does the IRS Form 990 have to be filed? It is dependent on the conclusion of your nonprofit's fiscal year. The IRS allows nonprofits to file using one of two methods: calendar year and fiscal year. **Calendar year** – A calendar tax year is 12 consecutive months beginning January 1 and ending December 31. **Fiscal year** – A fiscal tax year is 12 consecutive months ending on the last day of any month except December.

Nonprofits must file Forms 990, 990-EZ, 990-N, or 990-PF by the 15th day of the fifth month following the end of the accounting period. For example, if your accounting period is a calendar year with a close date of December 31, the due date is May 15. If your accounting period is a calendar year with a close date of June 30, the due date is November 15.

If last date of submission arrives at Saturday, Sunday, or any public holiday, the form is due on the next day following the holiday. The IRS will grant you two 90-day extensions if you need them, with the exception of Form 990-N filers. To change your tax year, an application form must be submitted to the IRS to make it official.

Nonprofits that fail to file their Form 990s for three years in a row will have their nonprofit status automatically revoked by the IRS. Revocation could result in additional costs, taxes, and paperwork for a nonprofit, and appeals are not an option.

Aside from the legal responsibilities and ramifications of managing Form 990, nonprofit boards should keep in mind that the annual filing serves a few other essential objectives. It's a document where the organization's mission is stated and the performance of programs and activities is tracked.

Nonprofit boards, as previously stated, have a responsibility to stay current on new legislation and regulations affecting nonprofit organizations. Form 990 was recently updated to require more information, such as conflict-of-interest disclosure, board and executive salaries, fraud, and other financial details. There's always the possibility that more modifications will occur.

Fines and Penalties

If the Form 990 return is filed after due date and the organization is unable to provide any reasonable grounds for late filing, a penalty of $20 per day will be charged after the due date. However, this penalty will not be more than the lower of 5% of total receipts or $10,000 of the entity during a tax year.

Organizations whose annual gross receipt exceed $1,000,000 will be liable for a fine of $100 per day following each missing day until submitted. Maximum penalty that can be charged up to one return is $50,000.

An organization that fails to file the required version of Form 990 information return for three consecutive tax years will automatically lose its tax-exempt status.

Regulations have provided an opportunity to request an abatement of penalties. It should be a written statement explaining reasonable cause for delay of submission. This declaration should be made by the appropriate authorized person of the nonprofit organization. It should include all necessary details for a reasonable cause of delay. This statement should be attached with Form 990.

When a request for the abatement of penalties is made for a reasonable cause, the statement should have all of its necessary supporting documents and it should address the followings items:

1. The reason why the penalty was imposed. For a late return filing or incomplete return filing or both, the daily delinquency penalty may be charged.

2. Explain why the organization failed to comply with regulatory requirements, including:

   - Reasons that prevented the organization from requesting an extension of time to return submission.

   - If the organization did not request an extension, explain how the organization was not acting carelessly or neglectfully.

   - Include necessary steps that organization will take to prevent occurrence of same situation in the future.

Reinstating a nonprofit's 501(c)3 exemption status retroactive

A nonprofit organization's tax-exempt status can be automatically revoked by the IRS. When this happens, the organization is no longer exempt from federal income tax, and almost all states will revoke the local tax-exemption, as well, by default. There are many reasons that the IRS may revoke an exemption status but the most common one is failure to file the IRS Form 990 annual return for three consecutive years.

If a tax-exempt organization has their exemption status revoked, serious issues arise around future donations and revenue being tax deductible. If the status is not restored, the organization will be liable for paying taxes due on all the income for the past three years as well.

Issues to consider with an automatic revocation:

- An automatic revocation is effective on the original filing due date of the third annual return or notice.

- Donors can deduct contributions made before an organization's name appears on the Automatic Revocation List.

- The IRS publishes the list of organizations whose tax-exempt status was automatically revoked because of failure to file any of the required Information Return Form 990s for three consecutive years.

- The organization will be required to file Form 1120 - U.S. Corporation Income Tax Return, due by the 15th day of the 3rd month after the end of an organization's tax year.

How To Get Your Tax Exemption Back

Reasonable Cause Statement. When re-applying for the tax-exempt status by completing Form 1023 again, a Reasonable Cause statement must be included with the application. The reasonable cause letter should be carefully drafted to show a detailed description of all the facts and circumstances regarding why the organization failed to file, how it discovered the failure, and the steps it has taken or will take to avoid or alleviate future failures. Most importantly it needs to establish that it was a non-willful act.

If there is a failure to sufficiently make a case, the organization will be responsible for past due taxes and the ruin of the organization.

There are three ways to reinstate your tax exemption status but they depend on the circumstances. Organizations have a chance to have their tax-exempt status reinstated to the date of revocation if they:

Complete and submit Form 1023 with the appropriate user fee.

- Include with the application a statement establishing that the organization had reasonable cause for its failure to file a required annual return for at least one of the three consecutive years in which it failed to file.

- Include with the application a statement confirming that it has filed required returns for those three years and for any other taxable years after such period and before the post-mark date of the application for which required returns were due and not filed.

- File properly completed and executed paper annual returns for the three consecutive years that caused the revocation and any following years.

There is only one opportunity for reinstatement of the tax-exempt status. It's imperative to get assistance from an attorney or a CPA to assist with the process. Even though the application the second time around is the same as applying for tax exemption the first time, there are several factors that are against you already. One of those factors may include that the organization failed to file for three consecutive years. And the second being the Reasonable Cause statement.

ORGANIZATIONAL RISK MANAGEMENT

What is risk management and why should an organization be concerned with it? Risk management is identifying potential risks in advance, analyzing them and taking precautionary steps to avoid potential risk to protect your organization from financial loss due to natural disasters and people's actions. Every organization should have a risk management plan in place and review it regularly to ensure, no matter what happens, that the organization's mission will be carried out.

The first step in risk management is to analyze your organization's assets and think through possible situations that may put them at risk. Nonprofits' assets can be categorized as follows:

- **People:** board members, volunteers, employees, clients, donors, and the public
- **Property:** buildings, furniture, equipment, supplies, copyrights, and trademarks
- **Income:** sales, fundraising, grants, and contributions
- **Goodwill:** reputation and stature in community the community.

The board of directors should create a risk management plan around its assets by considering questions like these:

- Would your organization close if a pandemic infected half the staff members?

- How would your organization survive if a hurricane or tornado destroyed the building where the organization's records are kept or provide services?

- Would a general downturn of the economy affect your organization?

- How would your organization be affected if a volunteer stole the organization's petty cash?

- What if a donor to your organization made a false statement to the press, destroying years of goodwill? Would the organization be able to stay in business and reestablish its good reputation?

These are some examples of possible risks that your organization should anticipate. Annually, all of the board members should set up a planning session and brainstorm other risks that may affect the organization. If the organization's work concerns health care or children, for example, being aware of the many state and federal laws, including safety laws, employment laws, and laws governing the service the organization provides is extremely important.

It's imperative for organizations to develop a useful risk management plan. The size of the organization isn't important. All organizations need a risk management plan to avoid financial loss.

Without one, an organization could be headed for trouble. A risk management plan will not prevent bad things from happening. But it will assist an organization in carrying out the mission and functioning if something does happen.

KEEPING THE NONPROFIT'S ASSETS SAFE

T he management and protection of financial resources must be a concern for all nonprofit organizations — from a small all-volunteer body to an established national association. Without sufficient financial resources, an organization is unable to achieve its mission and will struggle survive.

Physical Assets

When discussing financial risks, the focus is usually on the loss of money. However, most nonprofits have physical assets at risk as well. Organizations should also consider any office furniture, supplies, and equipment used to meet its mission is subject to loss. Hurricane, tornado, fire, or flood can damage or destroy the organization's physical assets. Also, an employee, volunteer, computer hacker, or other individuals seeking to harm the organization can steal or destroy its assets. In addition, loss of the supplies could have a detrimental effect on the organization's mission.

The best protection is systems, as well as policies and procedures, that limit the access to these assets. Computers contain a wealth of confidential information and data. Organizations should control and limit access to the people with a "need to know." Also, protect the organization's supplies and merchandise. Many organizations lose money on merchandise sales due to the lack of inventory and access controls.

One key to controlling financial management risks is the development and use of effective internal controls. Every nonprofit needs policies and procedures to control the access and use of its financial resources. The techniques involve general management controls and accounting controls.

Cash Assets

One of the most important assets of any nonprofit organization, or even a profit-oriented business, is the cash it earned, collected, or raised through its operations. Without cash, the organization would not be able to sustain itself or carry out the mission.

As a charity, there are many ways to generate the cash it needs in order to be able to achieve its missions, some of them include:

- Selling goods and services
- Fundraising events, such as roadshows, competitions, donation drives, etc.
- Grants
- Sponsorships
- Investments to achieve capital gain or receive dividends

The board of directors are held accountable for the operations and direction of the nonprofit organization. All money flowing in and out of the organization should be properly used, recorded, safeguarded, and budgeted.

Using the cash

The charity's money is collected from those who are in support of the charity's missions and visions. Hence, it is vital that such cash is spent wisely and in accordance with the charity's mission, governing documents, and policies.

A financial health check should be performed regularly to ensure that the charity has allocated its cash to its mission. Any deviation should immediately be investigated and corrected.

1) Operational expenses

There are always some out-of-pocket expenses that the board members or the employees will have to make in order to perform the duties. All such expenses can be claimed and reimbursed. They include:

- Telephone calls for charity work
- Reimbursable expenses (i.e., supplies, etc.)
- Travelling expenses incurred to travel to and from board meetings

A written policy must be established as a guideline. The policy should clearly state what the approved expenses are and how to claim, review, and approve such expenses.

As a board of director of a nonprofit, a fiduciary duty exists toward the charity's members, donors, corporate sponsors, grant makers, IRS, and the general public. The charity's best interest is always first above the board members and any matters that may give rise to a conflict of interests will be discussed by the board of directors.

2) Handling excess cash

On many occasions, the nonprofit may receive more donation or income than it initially had plans for or it spends much less than what was initially budgeted.

In situations like this, the charity should have a reserve policy that guides the organization as to what should be done with the excess cash. An assessment should also be carried out to determine if this extra money is reasonable.

Nonprofits should ensure that the annual report explains the policy and discloses the money it has in reserve (if any), where it is from, as well as how and when it will be utilized.

Recording the cash

Just like running a business, all the cash collected or received by the nonprofit should be well documented in the nonprofit's books and kept securely. Sufficient accounting records that are traceable must be maintained for every nonprofit.

All cash outflows should also be properly documented based on their purposes and amounts. In addition, be supported by relevant invoices or contracts signed with approved suppliers. Copies of the bank statements should be filed, as well, for reference.

Cash expenditures above a certain threshold should also be approved by the board of directors at board meetings. A copy of the meeting minutes should then be kept as a supporting document in the file or accounting records.

To ensure this is achievable, the nonprofit should make sure that it employs the right person with the right expertise to handle the accounting records. This person should have the knowledge to record the assets, liabilities, revenues, and expenses of the nonprofit per the applicable accounting standards.

Proper bookkeeping will also allow the board to know the financial position of the charity at one glance, which will be useful when the board needs to make an important decision that will rely on the financial status of the organization.

Note, accounting records should be kept for a specific period. Make sure you check the document retention list in the appendix to ensure compliance with the relevant laws and regulations.

Safeguarding the cash

The money received should be kept in a secured location, such as the bank. It is encouraged that a policy should be set up to ensure cash is deposited into the bank regularly.

The nonprofit should aim to keep its petty cash or cash on hand just sufficient for its day-to-day operations. This can lower the risk of theft.

To prevent misuse of cash, the organization should establish an authorization or approval based on the amount of cash to ensure every cash outflow is reviewed and approved before paid out.

As a best practice, the board of the nonprofit is advised to identify a list of risks in terms of safeguarding its cash. This will help determine the high-risk areas and allow such risks to be managed much more effectively. The risks should also be reviewed periodically to make sure they are up to date.

Budgeting the cash

When it comes to money, all nonprofits should set up a budget. A budget can aid in decision making and help ascertain that the organization's plans are reasonable, based on the money it has available. It also helps ensure that there is enough money to settle the bills as they become due.

The budget should detail how much cash that the nonprofit has now, how much it expects it will need in the coming year, and how much it plans to raise during the year.

Having a budget will allow for problems to be quickly seen before they arise and create action plans to handle them. Some of the actions that can be taken when there is a shortfall are:

- Increasing the fundraising activities
- Revising the plan by either stopping or delaying some activities to reduce planned spending

- Taking out a loan from banks or advances from board members
- Reviewing the expenses your charity incurs for services or facilities
- Discussing the issue with the grant bodies that provide the funds
- Merge with another charity
- Close your charity

All of the steps taken to prevent financial and other risks should be disclosed in the annual report to provide transparency to the stakeholders regarding what is being done to keep the organization's money safe.

UNDERSTANDING A NONPROFIT'S FINANCIAL HEALTH

E very nonprofit director and board member hopes for a huge endowment, cash reserves in the bank, and a surplus at the end of each year. Unfortunately, most of us are aware that this could be a fantasy rather than reality. How can you tell if an organization is financially strong without visible evidence of financial health?

Reserves and endowment balances aren't the only indicators of financial health. A huge budget or a complex accounting system does not automatically imply strong management and long-term success. The financial health of a nonprofit is dependent on management behavior – policies and procedures – just as it is dependent on a board members' personal health.

Even if there are occasional deficits or periods of tight cash flow, the characteristics listed below are solid indicators that an organization will be financially healthy in the long run.

- The board of directors and management are held accountable for long-term program and financial performance stability.
- Board members are aware of their financial tasks and duties.
- The board prepares and approves a realistic and well-considered budget.

- Budgets are created in tandem with program and operational planning.

- Management and the board of directors are committed to achieving an annual operating surplus.

- Qualified professionals generate and analyze consistent, accurate, and timely financial reports.

- Management and the board of directors keep a close eye on financial results in comparison to the budget and make adjustments to programs and activities as needed.

- Management carefully manages and oversees cash flow to ensure that obligations are met.

- Financial policies exist to develop, or have particular plans to develop, an operational reserve to cover cash deficits and program expansion.

- Major financial choices have policies in place, as well as proper and suitable internal controls.

- Management is dedicated to following all legal and funder reporting requirements.

- The board of directors and management examine short- and long-term plans on a regular basis, as well as define future goals and strategies.

CONCLUSION

Board of directors' orientations are a good place to begin talking about the fiduciary responsibilities. This gives the directors a foundation to have meaningful conversations about how their speech, actions and responsibilities affect the overall mission.

Board directors may already be practicing some things that directly coincide with their fiduciary responsibilities, whether they realize it or not. Some of the responsibilities are only necessary occasionally, so it's important for board of directors to consider situations that relate to their fiduciary duties so they can fulfill them responsibly all the time.

All board members should participate in some form of board development or training so that they have the necessary skills to read financial reports and make the best decisions for the organization. Some board of directors may need to improve their communication skills so they can maintain their independent viewpoints while working collaboratively with other board members.

Many nonprofit board members and employees have a for-profit or corporate background. A for-profit background may lay the foundation for reviewing and understanding financial statements and tax returns; nonprofit organizations have unique accounting and reporting distinctions that can complicate the mindset.

When considering the best way to report the organization's information either in the financial statements or via Form 990, consideration should be given to the readers of the information because they may have different nonfinancial objectives that can be shown through these reports. Donors and grantors want to ensure that the organization's mission is in alignment with their own values and goals. They may evaluate the governance structure and policies and procedures and are also likely interested in the organization's program accomplishments and community outreach and results. Board members and prospective board members will also be interested in the mission of the organization aligning with their personal values, but also from a fiduciary responsibility as well.

Fulfilling fiduciary duties means that boards should set policies and standards that ensure adequate internal controls. Clear policies will help boards measure the effectiveness of their activities, prevent fraud and designate financial responsibilities.

Board members' duty to the general public is to ensure the organization has the structures and policies in place to comply with all external requirements. Nonprofit organizations should balance these needs and wants of external parties when contemplating the setup of the financial statements and the reporting of the Form 990 in telling their unique story.

Ordinary and practical individuals get advice and guidance from outside experts when they need assistance in understanding issues that aren't familiar to them. In much the same way, board directors sometimes need to seek advice and guidance from experts who can help them understand the issues they face so that they can make informed decisions about the organization's activities.

APPENDICES

APPENDIX A: SAMPLE CONFLICT OF INTEREST POLICY...................... 173

APPENDIX B: DONOR ACKNOWLEDGEMENT TEMPLATES................. 180

APPENDIX C: COMPENSATION POLICY FOR OFFICERS, DIRECTORS, TOP MANAGEMENT OFFICIAL AND KEY EMPLOYEES 184

APPENDIX D: SAMPLE WHISTLEBLOWER POLICY 190

APPENDIX E: EXPENSE REIMBURSEMENT POLICY.................................... 193

APPENDIX F: BOARD OF DIRECTORS AND FINANCE COMMITTEE OVERSIGHT CHECKLIST... 196

APPENDIX G: DOCUMENT RETENTION POLICY 200

APPENDIX H: EXAMPLE NONPROFIT FINANCIAL STATEMENTS....... 203

APPENDIX A: SAMPLE CONFLICT OF INTEREST POLICY

Article I, Purpose

The purpose of the conflict-of-interest policy is to protect this tax-exempt organization's interest when it is contemplating entering into a transaction or arrangement that might benefit the private interest of an officer or director of the Organization or might result in a possible excess benefit transaction. This policy is intended to supplement but not replace any applicable state and federal laws governing conflict of interest applicable to nonprofit and charitable organizations.

Article II, Definitions

1. **Interested Person**

   Any director, principal officer, or member of a committee with governing board delegated powers, who has a direct or indirect financial interest, as defined below, is an interested person.

   If a person is an interested person with respect to any entity in the health care system of which the organization is a part, he or she is an interested person with respect to all entities in the health care system.]

2. Financial Interest

A person has a financial interest if the person has, directly or indirectly, through business, investment, or family:

    a. An ownership or investment interest in any entity with which the Organization has a transaction or arrangement,

    b. A compensation arrangement with the Organization or with any entity or individual with which the Organization has a transaction or arrangement, or

    c. A potential ownership or investment interest in, or compensation arrangement with, any entity or individual with which the Organization is negotiating a transaction or arrangement. Compensation includes direct and indirect remuneration as well as gifts or favors that are not insubstantial.

A financial interest is not necessarily a conflict of interest. Under Article III, Section 2, a person who has a financial interest may have a conflict of interest only if the appropriate governing board or committee decides that a conflict of interest exists.

Article III , Procedures

1. Duty to Disclose.

In connection with any actual or possible conflict of interest, an interested person must disclose the existence of the financial interest and be given the opportunity to disclose all material facts to the directors and members of committees with governing board delegated powers considering the proposed transaction or arrangement.

2. **Determining Whether a Conflict of Interest Exists**

   After disclosure of the financial interest and all material facts, and after any discussion with the interested person, he/she shall leave the governing board or committee meeting while the determination of a conflict of interest is discussed and voted upon. The remaining board or committee members shall decide if a conflict of interest exists.

3. **Procedures for Addressing the Conflict of Interest**

   a. An interested person may make a presentation at the governing board or committee meeting, but after the presentation, he/she shall leave the meeting during the discussion of, and the vote on, the transaction or arrangement involving the possible conflict of interest.

   b. The chairperson of the governing board or committee shall, if appropriate, appoint a disinterested person or committee to investigate alternatives to the proposed transaction or arrangement.

   c. After exercising due diligence, the governing board or committee shall determine whether the Organization can obtain with reasonable efforts a more advantageous transaction or arrangement from a person or entity that would not give rise to a conflict of interest.

d. If a more advantageous transaction or arrangement is not reasonably possible under circumstances not producing a conflict of interest, the governing board or committee shall determine by a majority vote of the disinterested directors whether the transaction or arrangement is in the Organization's best interest, for its own benefit, and whether it is fair and reasonable. In conformity with the above determination it shall make its decision as to whether to enter into the transaction or arrangement.

4. Violations of the Conflicts of Interest Policy

a. If the governing board or committee has reasonable cause to believe a member has failed to disclose actual or possible conflicts of interest, it shall inform the member of the basis for such belief and afford the member an opportunity to explain the alleged failure to disclose.

b. If, after hearing the member's response and after making further investigation as warranted by the circumstances, the governing board or committee determines the member has failed to disclose an actual or possible conflict of interest, it shall take appropriate disciplinary and corrective action.

Article IV, Records of Proceedings

The minutes of the governing board and all committees with board delegated powers shall contain:

a. The names of the persons who disclosed or otherwise were found to have a financial interest in connection with an actual or possible conflict of interest, the nature of the financial interest, any action taken to determine whether a conflict of interest was present, and the governing board's or committee's decision as to whether a conflict of interest in fact existed.

b. The names of the persons who were present for discussions and votes relating to the transaction or arrangement, the content of the discussion, including any alternatives to the proposed transaction or arrangement, and a record of any votes taken in connection with the proceedings.

Article V, Compensation

a. A voting member of the governing board who receives compensation, directly or indirectly, from the Organization for services is precluded from voting on matters pertaining to that member's compensation.

b. A voting member of any committee whose jurisdiction includes compensation matters and who receives compensation, directly or indirectly, from the Organization for services is precluded from voting on matters pertaining to that member's compensation.

c. No voting member of the governing board or any committee whose jurisdiction includes compensation matters and who receives compensation, directly or indirectly, from the Organization, either individually or collectively, is prohibited from providing information to any committee regarding compensation.

Article VI, Annual Statements

Each director, principal officer and member of a committee with governing board delegated powers shall annually sign a statement which affirms such person:

a. Has received a copy of the conflicts of interest policy,

b. Has read and understands the policy,

c. Has agreed to comply with the policy, and

d. Understands the Organization is charitable and in order to maintain its federal tax exemption it must engage primarily in activities which accomplish one or more of its tax- exempt purposes.

Article VII, Periodic Reviews

To ensure the Organization operates in a manner consistent with charitable purposes and does not engage in activities that could jeopardize its tax-exempt status, periodic reviews shall be conducted. The periodic reviews shall, at a minimum, include the following subjects:

a. Whether compensation arrangements and benefits are reasonable, based on competent survey information, and the result of arm's length bargaining.

b. Whether partnerships, joint ventures, and arrangements with management organizations conform to the Organization's written policies, are properly recorded, reflect reasonable investment or payments for goods and services, further charitable purposes and do not result in inurement, impermissible private benefit or in an excess benefit transaction.

Article VIII, Use of Outside Experts

When conducting the periodic reviews as provided for in Article VII, the Organization may, but need not, use outside advisors. If outside experts are used, their use shall not relieve the governing board of its responsibility for ensuring periodic reviews are conducted.

APPENDIX B: DONOR ACKNOWLEDGEMENT
TEMPLATES

Cash Contribution

6/30/20XX (Date of letter to donor)

Dear Robert and Rolanda,

Thank you for your contribution to [Your Organization Name] in support of our mission to provide _____ and _____ services that help charitable organizations be more effective. We received your contribution on

January 24, 20XX in the amount of $XXX

No goods or services were provided to you by [Your Organization Name] in return for your contribution.

[Your Organization Name] is recognized as a tax-exempt organization under section 501(c)(3) of the Internal Revenue Code. Contributions to organizations with 501(c)(3) status may be tax deductible. Please consult your tax advisor to determine deductibility of this contribution. This letter is your receipt for income tax purposes.

Sincerely,

[Your Organization Name]

Non-Cash Property Contribution

1/30/20XX (Date of letter to donor)

Dear Robert and Rolanda,

Thank you for your contribution of [property, used equipment, publicly traded securities and/or virtual currencies], which is described below, to [Your Organization Name] in support of our mission to provide _____ and_____ services that help charitable organizations be more effective. On January 24, 20XX, we received your contribution of:

- [Item 1]
- [Item 2]
- [Item 3]

No goods or services were provided to you by [Your Organization Name] in return for your contribution.

[Your Organization Name] is recognized as a tax-exempt organization under section 501(c)(3) of the Internal Revenue Code. Contributions to organizations with 501(c)(3) status may be tax deductible. Please consult your tax advisor to determine deductibility of this contribution. This letter is your receipt for income tax purposes.

Sincerely,

[Your Organization Name]

Donated Services or Use of Facilities

1/30/20XX (Date of letter to donor)

Dear Robert and Rolanda,

Thank you for your donation of [describe donated services or use of facilities] on January 24, 20XX [or during the period of January 1, 20XX through June 30, 20XX] to [Your Organization Name] in support of our mission to provide advisory and training services that help charitable organizations be more effective.

No goods or services were provided to you by [Your Organization Name] in return for your contribution.

[Your Organization Name] is recognized as a tax-exempt organization under section 501(c)(3) of the Internal Revenue Code. Contributions to organizations with 501(c)(3) status may be tax deductible. There are specific rules affecting the deductibility of donated services (or donated use of facilities), and we recommend that you consult your tax advisor to determine deductibility of this contribution, including any related out of pocket expenses. This letter is your receipt for income tax purposes.

Sincerely,

[Your Organization Name]

Quid Pro Quo Donation Example

{Note: This disclosure can also be made on a solicitation, ticket, or other receipt or evidence of payment furnished to the purchaser}

December 15, 20XX (Date of letter to donor)

Dear Rolanda,

Thank you for your purchase of two tickets to our upcoming fundraising banquet and silent auction at $200 each, totaling $400. Admission includes dinner with an estimated value of $50. The amount of a contribution that is deductible for federal income tax purposes is limited to the amount contributed, reduced by the value of any goods or services provided by the organization. Accordingly, $300 of each admission is eligible for an income tax deduction.

Thank you again for your support of this event.

Sincerely,

[Your Organization Name]

APPENDIX C: COMPENSATION POLICY FOR OFFICERS, DIRECTORS, TOP MANAGEMENT OFFICIAL AND KEY EMPLOYEES

Article I. Policy and Purposes

It is the policy of ORGANIZATION (the "organization") that all compensation paid by the organization is reasonable based upon a review of comparability information.] This policy provides a procedure for the review and approval of the compensation of the officers, directors [trustees], CEO, executive director or top management official, and key employees of the organization ("Compensated Individuals") consistent with applicable federal tax law and state law.

Article II. Procedure for Approval of Compensation

1. **General.** The board of directors or trustees, or authorized committee ("Governing Body") shall review and approve the compensation of Compensated Individuals.

2. **Specific Requirements.** The Governing Body reviewing and approving compensation for Compensated Individuals shall satisfy the following requirements or procedures:

    a. **Approval by Persons Without a Conflict of Interest.** Compensation shall be reviewed and approved by the Governing Body, provided that persons with a conflict of interest with respect to the compensation arrangement at issue are not involved.

Members of the Governing Body do not have a
conflict of interest if they (a) are not benefitting from
or participating in the compensation arrangement; (b)
are not in an employment relationship subject to the
direction or control of any person benefitting from or
participating in the compensation arrangement; (c) do
not receive compensation or other payments subject to
the approval of any person benefitting from or
participating in the compensation arrangement; (d)
have no material financial interest affected by the
compensation arrangement; and (e) do not approve a
transaction providing economic benefits to any person
participating in the compensation arrangement, who in
turn has or will approve a transaction providing
economic benefits to the member.

b. **Use of Comparability Data.** In its review and
approval of compensation, the Governing Body shall
review and use data and surveys of comparable
compensation for similarly qualified persons in
functionally comparable positions at similarly situated
organizations.

c. **Recording Compensation Deliberations.** The
Governing Body shall contemporaneously document
and maintain records with respect to the deliberations
and decisions regarding the compensation
arrangement.

185

d. **Review and Approval for Certain Executive Officers.** In addition to the requirements of this policy applicable to all Compensated Individuals, any compensation set for the CEO or president, and CFO or treasurer, (or individuals with equivalent powers, duties or responsibilities comparable to these positions), must also be determined to be just and reasonable. The Governing Body's review and approval shall occur initially upon hiring, whenever the term of employment, if any, is renewed or extended, and whenever the compensation is modified. Separate review and approval shall not be required if a modification of compensation extends to substantially all employees.

1. **Specific Requirements.** The Governing Body reviewing and approving compensation for Compensated Individuals shall satisfy the following requirements or procedures:

   a. **Approval by Persons Without a Conflict of Interest.** Compensation shall be reviewed and approved by the Governing Body, provided that persons with a conflict of interest with respect to the compensation arrangement at issue are not involved. Members of the Governing Body do not have a conflict of interest if they (a) are not benefitting from or participating in the compensation arrangement; (b) are not in an employment relationship subject to the direction or control of any person benefitting from or participating in the compensation arrangement; (c) do not receive compensation or other payments subject to the approval of any person benefitting from or participating in the compensation arrangement; (d) have no material financial interest affected by the compensation arrangement; and (e) do not approve a transaction providing economic benefits to any person participating in the compensation arrangement, who in turn has or will approve a transaction providing economic benefits to the member.

b. **Use of Comparability Data.** In its review and approval of compensation, the Governing Body shall affirmatively determine that compensation is reasonable to the organization based upon information sufficient to determine whether the value of services is the amount that would ordinarily be paid for like services by like enterprises, whether taxable or tax exempt, under like circumstances. Relevant information includes, but is not limited to, compensation levels paid by similarly situated organizations, both taxable and tax exempt, for functionally comparable positions; the availability of similar services in the geographic area of the organization; current compensation surveys compiled by independent firms; and actual written offers from similar institutions competing for the services of the compensated person. If the organization has average annual gross receipts of less than $1 million for the prior three tax years, the Governing Body will have appropriate comparability information if it has information on compensation paid by three comparable organizations in the same or similar communities for similar services.

c. **Recording Compensation Deliberations.** The Governing Body's review and approval of compensation shall be promptly recorded in the minutes of its meetings and contain: (a) the terms of the compensation and the date approved; (b) the names of the members of the Governing Body who were present during the discussion and those who voted on the approved compensation; (c) the comparability data obtained and relied upon, and how it was obtained; (d) any action taken with respect to consideration of the compensation by a member of the Governing Body who had a conflict of interest with respect to the compensation; and (e) if the reasonable compensation is higher or lower than the range of comparability data obtained, the basis for the decision. Such minutes shall be reviewed and approved by the Governing Body as reasonable, accurate and complete within a reasonable time after the review and approval of the compensation.

d. **Review and Approval for Certain Executive Officers.** In addition to the requirements of this policy applicable to all Compensated Individuals, any compensation set for the CEO or president, and CFO or treasurer, (or individuals with equivalent powers, duties or responsibilities comparable to these positions), must be determined to be just and reasonable. The Governing Body's review and approval shall occur initially upon hiring, whenever the term of employment, if any, is renewed or extended, and whenever the compensation is modified. Separate review and approval shall not be required if a modification of compensation extends to substantially all employees.

APPENDIX D: SAMPLE WHISTLEBLOWER POLICY

[Your Organization Name] encourages its employees to report improper activities in the workplace and will protect employees from retaliation for making any such report in good faith.

1. **Employee Rights**

   Employees have the right to report, without suffering retaliation, any activity by [Your Organization Name] or any of our employees that the employee reasonably believes: 1) violates any state or federal law; 2) violates or amounts to noncompliance with a state or federal rule or regulation; or 3) violates fiduciary responsibilities by a nonprofit corporation. In addition, employees can refuse to participate in an activity that would result in a violation of state or federal statutes, or a violation or noncompliance with a state or federal rule or regulation.

   Employees are also protected from retaliation for having exercised any of these rights in any former employment.

   The whistleblower protection laws do not entitle employees to violate a confidential privilege of [Your Organization Name] (such as the attorney-client privilege) or improperly disclose trade-secret information.

2. **Where to Report**

   Employees have the duty to comply with all applicable laws and to assist [Your Organization Name] to ensure legal compliance. An employee who suspects a problem with legal compliance is required to report the situation(s) to the Executive Director or Chair of the Board of Directors if the complaint involves the Executive Director.

   Employees may also report information regarding possible unlawful activity to an appropriate government or law enforcement agency.

3. **Protection from Retaliation**

   It is the intent of this policy to encourage employees to report fraudulent or illegal activities and there shall be no retaliation for any reports made pursuant to this policy. Any employee who believes they have been retaliated against for whistle blowing may file a complaint with either the Executive Director or the Chair of the Board of Directors. Any complaint of retaliation will be promptly investigated and remedial action taken when warranted. This protection from retaliation is not intended to prohibit managers or supervisors from taking action, including disciplinary action, in the ordinary course of business based on valid performance-related factors.

Please sign below to confirm you have read and understand the Whistleblower policy:

_____   _____

Employee Signature   Date

_____

Employee's typed or printed name

cc: Employee, Personnel File

APPENDIX E: EXPENSE REIMBURSEMENT POLICY

Article I, Purpose

The purpose of the Expense Reimbursement Policy is to protect this tax-exempt organization's [Your Organization Name] non-profit status by providing operating procedures for reimbursement of valid, [Your Organization Name] business expenses. This policy addresses advance payment request, reimbursement payment request, and travel advance request. To ensure appropriate financial controls and approvals are in place, all [Your Organization Name] expenses will follow these procedures. This policy is intended to supplement but not replace any applicable state and federal laws governing nonprofit and charitable organizations.

Article II, Definitions

1. **Expense.** Any payable item directly related to and caused by operational activities of the [Your Organization Name]. Expenses must be directly or indirectly related to the mission of [Your Organization Name].

2. **Member.** Only active members (see Bylaws) acting on behalf of the [Your Organization Name] and executing [Your Organization Name] business may submit advance payment requests, expense reimbursement request, or travel advance request.

3. **Request Types**

   a. *Advance Payment Request (Check Request) Form* is submitted when the [Your Organization Name] expense, vendor and amount are known sufficiently in advance to secure an advance payment via [Your Organization Name] check.

   b. *Expense Reimbursement Request* is submitted after a pre-approved [Your Organization Name] expense has been paid by a member. Whether the member chooses to donate the expense amount or not, an Expense Reimbursement Request Form will be submitted for all valid [Your Organization Name] expenses.

   c. *Travel Advance Request* is submitted only when pre-approved [Your Organization Name] related travel is authorized and individual funds are not available to pre-fund the travel expense. All travel related receipts must be received within 10 business days of trip completion.

4. **Authorization.** All [Your Organization Name] related expenses are authorized either by the annual budget process or, by the Board of Directors. Only the President, Vice President or Secretary of the [Your Organization Name] may authorize payments. The Treasurer may not solely authorize payment.

5. **Timing.** Expenses must be turned into the Treasurer for reimbursement no later than 30 days from expenditure date except at year-end when all late December expenses must be submitted by January 15th of the succeeding year. This ensures sufficient timing to close [Your Organization Name] financial books for State and Federal regulatory reporting and audit requirements. Valid [Your Organization Name] expenses submitted after the above dates will not be reimbursed.

APPENDIX F: BOARD OF DIRECTORS AND FINANCE COMMITTEE OVERSIGHT CHECKLIST

The Board of Directors and/or Executive Director responsibilities:

- ☐ Limit the number of individuals that can sign checks for the organization.

- ☐ Open a business banking/checking account in the organization's name.

- ☐ Establish internal accounting systems, including checks and balances, so one staff member does not have total control over finances.

- ☐ Ensure maintenance of accurate records of all income, expenditures, transactions, and activities throughout the year.

- ☐ Develop annual budgets that provide clear direction for all organizational spending.

- ☐ Prepare financial statements for quarterly review by the board. Statements should include balance sheet, profit and loss with a comparison to budget and a cash flow forecast.

- ☐ Ask the Treasurer of the organization to perform an independent inspection of the key records (bank statements, investment statements, bank reconciliations, credit card statements and Executive Director expense report) on a regular basis (quarterly).

☐ File appropriate annual reports with the IRS and State; almost all charitable nonprofits that are recognized as tax-exempt by the IRS are required to file an annual report with the IRS, known as the "Form 990."

☐ Comply with a conflict-of-interest policy; review and sign the policy.

☐ Make an annual fundraising plan.

The Board of Directors and/or Executive Committee responsibilities:

☐ Know the names of individuals that can sign checks for the organization.

☐ Know all financial institutions that hold the nonprofit's assets.

☐ Know the name(s) listed on any bank accounts for the organization.

☐ Know if the organization has borrowed money and the terms of the loan(s).

☐ Ensure the organization has financial checks and balances.

☐ Review and approve any and all compensation paid to the Executive Director.

☐ Maintain and review a conflict-of-interest policy; review and sign the policy.

☐ Look over financial reports quarterly or monthly.

☐ Approve annual budgets.

- ☐ Confirm annual filings; review the Form 990 prior to filing with the IRS.

- ☐ Review and discuss the independent financial audit (if applicable).

- ☐ Review the annual fundraising plan.

- ☐ Serve without payment unless the organization has a policy for reimbursable out-of-pocket expenses.

- ☐ Review insurance coverages to ensure risk of loss is properly mitigated and ensure insurance policies are renewed.

- ☐ Have a written policy prohibiting employees and members of employees' immediate families from serving as board chair or treasurer.

- ☐ Oversee investments and reinvest assets when appropriate.

- ☐ Insist on the best value for goods and services through comparisons and an informed bidding process.

- ☐ Disclose any related party transactions between board members or their family, to the board of directors, the Internal Revenue Service and the auditor.

- ☐ Keep minutes of board meetings that reflect: the date, time and place of the meeting; what directors (and others) were present and whether this made a quorum; what items were submitted for a vote; and who voted for, against, or abstained; and any other information to fulfill legal obligations.

- ☐ Approve the expense reports of the Executive Director.

☐ Establish a cash management policy that dictates an appropriate level of reserves and a plan for establishing a reserve fund and the process for drawing funds from reserves.

☐ Understand and approve key contracts/commitments entered into by the organization.

☐ Perform a review of organizational risks to ensure understanding of operational risks including, but not limited to: reliance on single key employee, funder, event or vendor, liabilities associated with delivering programming, risks associated with long term contracts.

APPENDIX G: DOCUMENT RETENTION POLICY

Accounts payable ledgers and schedules: 10 years

Accounts receivable ledgers and schedules: 10 years

Audit reports of accountants: Permanently

Bank statements: 10 years

Capital stock and bond records: ledgers, transfer payments, stubs showing issues, record of interest coupon, options, etc.: Permanently

Cash books: 10 years

Checks (canceled, with exception below): 10 years

Checks (canceled, for important payments; i.e., taxes, purchase of property, special contracts, etc. --checks should be filed with the papers pertaining to the underlying transaction): Permanently

Contracts and leases (expired): 10 years

Contracts and leases still in effect: Permanently

Correspondence, general: 4 years

Correspondence (legal and important matters): Permanently

Depreciation schedules: 10 years

Donation records of endowment funds and of significant restricted funds: Permanently

Donation records, other: 10 years

***Note:** Donation records include a written agreement between the donor and the charity with regard to any contribution, an email communication or notes of or recordings of an oral discussion between the charity and the donor where the representative of the charity made representations to the donor with regard to the contribution on which the donor may have relied in making the gift.

Duplicate deposit slips: 10 years

Employee personnel records (after termination): 7 years

Employment applications: 3 years

Expense analyses and expense distribution schedules (includes allowance and reimbursement of employees, officers, etc., for travel and other expenses: 10 years

Financial statements (end-of-year): Permanently

General ledgers and end-of-year statements: Permanently

Insurance policies (expired): Permanently

Insurance records, current accident reports, claims, policies, etc.: Permanently

Internal reports, miscellaneous: 3 years

Inventories of products, materials, supplies: 10 years

Invoices to customers: 10 years

Invoices from vendors: 10 years

Journals: 10 years

Minute books of Board of Directors, including Bylaws and Articles of Incorporation: Permanently

Payroll records and summaries, including payments to pensioners: 10 years

Purchase orders: 3 years

Sales records: 10 years

Scrap and salvage records: 10 years

Subsidiary ledgers: 10 years

Tax returns and worksheets, revenue agents' reports, and other documents relating to determination of tax liability: Permanently

Time sheets and cards: 10 years

Voucher register and schedules: 10 years

Volunteer records: 3 years

Warning: All permitted document destruction shall be halted if the organization is being investigated by a governmental law enforcement agency, and routine destruction shall not be resumed without the written approval of legal counsel or the Chief Executive Officer.

APPENDIX H: EXAMPLE NONPROFIT FINANCIAL STATEMENTS

ABC, INC.
STATEMENTS OF FINANCIAL POSITION
June 30, 20XX and 20XX

	20XX	20XX
ASSETS		
Cash and cash equivalents	$ 29,907	$ 15,655
Short-term investments	62,378	24,833
Accounts receivable	—	1,355
Prepaid expenses	6,402	8,845
Unconditional promises to give	198,188	190,304
Cash restricted to purchase of equipment	30,000	—
Long-term investments	64,875	13,282
Contribution receivable—charitable Lead trust	206,800	230,000
Deposits on leased and other property	1,000	1,500
Property and equipment	648,410	664,342
TOTAL ASSETS	$ 1,247,960	$ 1,150,116
LIABILITIES		
Accounts payable	$ —	$ 3,445
Compensation	4,284	8,145
Refundable advances	2,132	—
Long-term debt	79,991	85,930
TOTAL LIABILITIES	86,407	97,520
NET ASSETS		
Unrestricted		
Designated for new program development	50,000	—
Undesignated	612,559	612,499
Temporarily restricted	492,125	435,932
Permanently restricted	6,869	4,165
TOTAL NET ASSETS	1,161,553	1,052,596
TOTAL LIABILITIES AND NET ASSETS	$ 1,247,960	$ 1,150,116

ABC, INC.
STATEMENT OF ACTIVITIES
Year Ended June 30, 20XX

	Unrestricted	Temporarily Restricted	Permanently Restricted	Total
REVENUES, GAINS, AND OTHER SUPPORT				
Contributions				
United Way Services	$ —	$ 156,275	$ —	$ 156,275
Women's shelter	—	46,193	—	46,193
Capital campaign	—	4,771	—	4,771
Equipment acquisition	—	30,000	—	30,000
Endowment	—	—	2,704	2,704
Other	89,736	—	—	89,736
Federal financial assistance	43,473	—	—	43,473
Program service fees	22,417	—	—	22,417
Investment return	5,766	497	—	6,263
Change in value of split-interest agreement	—	1,800	—	1,800
Other	2,777	—	—	2,777
Net assets released from restrictions				
Expiration of time restriction—Red Cross Services	146,465	(146,465)	—	—
Restrictions satisfied by charitable lead trust receipts				
Restrictions satisfied by payments	25,000	(25,000)	—	—
TOTAL REVENUES, GAINS, AND OTHER SUPPORT	11,878	(11,878)	=	=
	347,512	56,193	2,704	406,409
EXPENSES				
Program services				
Women and children	134,051	—	—	134,051
Men	94,231	—	—	94,231
Supporting services		—		
Management and general	55,629		—	55,629
Fund-raising	13,541	=	=	13,541
TOTAL EXPENSES	297,452	=	=	297,452
CHANGE IN NET ASSETS	50,060	56,193	2,704	108,957
NET ASSETS AT BEGINNING OF YEAR	612,499	435,932	4,165	1,052,596
NET ASSETS AT END OF YEAR	$ 662,559	$ 492,125	$ 6,869	$ 1,161,553

ABC, INC.
STATEMENT OF FUNCTIONAL EXPENSES
Year Ended June 30, 20XX

	Program Services		Supporting Services		
	Women and Children	Me	Management and General	Fund-raising	Total
Compensation and related expenses					
Compensation					
Full-time	$ 27,530	$ 26,049	$ 31,579	$ 7,894	$ 93,052
Part-time	42,531	41,316	7,141	—	90,988
Employee benefits	2,020	1,010	861	189	4,080
Medical	94	108	254	43	499
Other Payroll taxes	5,354	5,200	2,926	731	14,211
	77,529	73,683	42,761	8,857	202,830
Conferences and training	215	144	502	—	861
Depreciation	20,644	—	2,534	634	23,812
Food	3,039	76	—	—	3,115
Insurance					
Property and casualty	1,295	515	—	—	1,810
Vehicles	3,785	—	—	—	3,785
Worker's compensation	—	—	1,548	387	1,935
Interest	—	—	248	—	248
Maintenance of equipment	324	—	733	—	1,057
Occupancy					
Electricity Gas	10,964	1,715	975	243	13,897
Heating oil	1,081	601	105	15	1,802
Maintenance	—	2,054	—	—	2,054
Rent	3,449	938	371	24	4,782
Water and sewer	—	8,388	—	—	8,388
Postage	1,502	1,282	135	32	2,951
Printing	68	39	997	996	2,100
Specific assistance	434	138	968	1,450	2,990
	1,012	274	—	—	1,286
Supplies					
Cleaning	3,271	2,243	—	—	5,514
Office	357	365	1,779	432	2,933
Other	971	14	303	27	1,315
Telephone	2,293	874	581	387	4,135
Transportation					
Fuel	409	208	—	—	617
Repairs and other	1,385	680	869	—	2,934
Other	24	—	220	57	301
	$ 134,051	$ 94,231	$ 55,629	$ 13,541	$ 297,452

ABC, INC.
STATEMENTS OF CASH FLOWS
Years Ended June 30, 20XX and 20XX

	20XX	20XX
CASH FLOWS FROM OPERATING ACTIVITIES		
Increase in net assets	$ 108,957	$ 461,356
Adjustments to reconcile increase in net assets to net cash provided by operating activities:		
Depreciation	23,812	14,787
Amortization of discount on split-interest agreement	(1,800)	—
Donated vehicle included in contributions	—	(837)
Unrealized gains on investments	(3,256)	(192)
(Increase) decrease in operating assets:		
Accounts receivable	1,355	(677)
Prepaid expenses	2,443	(1,169)
Unrestricted unconditional promises to give	5,748	(2,874)
United Way Services funding for the next fiscal year	(19,682)	(5,563)
Contributions receivable—charitable lead trust	25,000	(230,000)
Increase (decrease) in operating liabilities:		
Accounts payable	(3,445)	300
Compensation	(3,861)	354
Refundable advances	2,132	—
Contributions restricted for long-term purposes:		
Contributions	(79,897)	(195,082)
Amortization of discount on unconditional promises to give	(3,771)	(4,827)
NET CASH PROVIDED BY OPERATING ACTIVITIES	53,735	35,576
CASH FLOWS FROM INVESTING ACTIVITIES		
Short-term investments, net	(37,545)	(13,982)
Purchases of long-term investments	(60,837)	(22,749)
Proceeds from maturity of long-term investments	12,500	11,000
Payments for property and equipment	(2,129)	(501,365)
Purchase of assets restricted to investment in property and equipment	(30,000)	—
Other	—	(500)
NET CASH USED BY INVESTING ACTIVITIES	(118,011)	(527,596)
CASH FLOWS FROM FINANCING ACTIVITIES		
Collections of contributions restricted for long-term purposes:		
Capital Campaign	17,771	362,946
Women's shelter	39,243	—
Purchase of equipment	30,000	—
Endowment	2,704	4,165
Payments on First Bank note	(876)	—
Payments on SBA note	(10,314)	(10,314)
NET CASH PROVIDED BY FINANCING ACTIVITIES	78,528	356,797
NET INCREASE (DECREASE) IN CASH AND CASH EQUIVALENTS	14,252	(135,223)
BEGINNING CASH AND CASH EQUIVALENTS	15,655	150,878
ENDING CASH AND CASH EQUIVALENTS	$ 29,907	$ 15,655

Noncash investing and financing activities in 20XX consist of financing the cost of acquiring a copier through a long-term note of $5,251, payable to First Bank. There were no such activities in 20XX.

206

ABOUT THE AUTHOR

Rolanda S. McDuffie, CPA, is a native of Tampa. She attended North Carolina Agricultural & Technical State University where she earned a Bachelor's degree in Accounting. Ms. McDuffie continued her education by obtaining a MBA, with a concentration in Computer Resources and Information Management, as well as a Master's in Accounting & Finance.

Ms. McDuffie manages a successful full-service CPA firm that she started over eight years ago. Her professional passion is to assist non-profit organizations and help small business owners grow and become financially fit through the use of accounting, tax, investing, and business advisory services. That same passion is what drives her to serve the community in various, related capacities. In addition to running a CPA firm, she is also an adjunct professor, teaching accounting, business, and software training courses. Ms. McDuffie is also frequently called upon to provide her expertise at workshops, seminars, and conferences. She currently serves on the Board of Directors of several non-profit organizations and provides her expertise in various capacities to different nonprofit organizations all over the United States.

Made in the USA
Las Vegas, NV
03 October 2023

78527321R00118